Best of Country Cakes

Cakes Considered "a Cut Above" Make Any Occasion Special

CAKES traditionally mark the special events in our lives, from birthdays and graduations to weddings and anniversaries. They also add a festive touch to holiday meals throughout the year and make scrumptious desserts for casual weeknight suppers and fancier company dinners.

Whether the occasion calls for crowd-pleasing sheet cakes, pretty layered cakes, elegant cake rolls, light and airy tube cakes, buttery pound cakes, individual cupcakes, fruity upside-down cakes or fun-shaped cakes, we have them all in this *Best of Country Cakes* book—and more!

There are 170 classic cake recipes contained in the pages of this brand-new cookbook. It's chock-full of the most-requested cake recipes from past issues of *Taste of Home* magazine and its "sister" publications.

You can make these recipes with confidence because each and every one is a tried-and-true favorite of a fellow cook's family. Our Test Kitchen staff prepared and taste-tasted each cake as well, selecting it for a book we're proud to call "The Best".

Helpful tips we've sprinkled throughout the cookbook will serve as a guide when making any of these beautiful cakes. You'll learn which kinds of pans are best for baking cakes, tips for cooling, cutting and storing cakes, and so much more. We've also included full-color photos of most cakes, so you can see what they look like before you start baking.

So go ahead and bake any of the 170 fabulous cakes featured in this *Best of Country Cakes* book. Any way you slice it, they'll make any occasion extra special.

Editor: Jean Steiner
Art Directors: Judy Larson, Niki Malmberg
Food Editor: Janaan Cunningham
Associate Food Editors: Coleen Martin, Diane Werner
Senior Recipe Editor: Sue A. Jurack
Associate Editors: Julie Schnittka, Heidi Reuter Lloyd
Food Photography: Rob Hagen, Dan Roberts
Senior Food Photography Artist: Stephanie Marchese
Food Photography Artist: Julie Ferron
Photo Studio Manager: Anne Schimmel
Graphic Art Associates: Ellen Lloyd, Catherine Fletcher
Chairman and Founder: Roy Reiman
President: Russell Denson

©2003 Reiman Media Group, Inc.
5400 S. 60th St., Greendale WI 53129
International Standard Book Number: 0-89821-379-7
Library of Congress Control Number: 2003091378

Best of Country Cakes

p. 6

p. 22

p. 20

p. 22

p. 23

Clockwise from top left: Lemon Meringue Cake, Orange Cream Cake, Chocolate Creme Cakes, Banana Fudge Cake and Praline Ice Cream Cake.

Snack & Single Layer Cakes

Lemon Meringue Cake

Debra Blair, Glenwood, Minnesota

(Pictured above and on page 4)

My husband likes lemon meringue pie, so I figured this would appeal to him. It's become his favorite dessert.

   1/4 cup butter *or* margarine, softened
   1/2 cup sugar
      1 egg plus 2 egg yolks
      1 cup all-purpose flour
      1 teaspoon baking powder
   1/3 cup milk
   1/2 teaspoon vanilla extract
FILLING:
      2 egg yolks
      1 cup water
   3/4 cup sugar
   1/3 cup all-purpose flour
   1/2 teaspoon grated lemon peel
   1/4 cup fresh lemon juice
      1 tablespoon butter *or* margarine
MERINGUE:
      4 egg whites, room temperature
   1/2 teaspoon cream of tartar
   1/2 cup sugar

In a mixing bowl, cream butter and sugar. Add egg and yolks; mix well. Combine flour and baking powder; add to creamed mixture alternately with milk. Mix well. Add vanilla. Pour into greased and floured 9-in. round baking pan. Bake at 350° for 25-30 minutes or until a toothpick inserted near center comes out clean. Cool in pan 10 minutes; remove to wire rack and cool completely.

In a heavy saucepan, combine egg yolks, water, sugar, flour and peel; bring to a gentle boil over medium heat, stirring constantly. Cook and stir for 2-3 minutes or until thickened. Remove from the heat. Stir in lemon juice and butter. Place cake on a baking sheet; spoon filling on top of cake up to 1/2 in. from edge.

Beat egg whites until foamy. Add cream of tartar; beat on high for 1 minute. Add sugar, 1 tablespoon at a time, beating well after each addition. Beat until stiff peaks form, about 3 minutes. Carefully spread over filling, sealing to edges of cake. Bake at 350° for 12-15 minutes or until lightly browned. **Yield:** 6-8 servings.

Mississippi Mud Cake

Tammi Simpson, Greensburg, Kentucky

(Pictured below)

Make this tempting cake, and you'll satisfy kids of all ages! A fudgy brownie-like base is topped with marshmallow creme and a nutty frosting.

      1 cup butter *or* margarine, softened
      2 cups sugar
      4 eggs
1-1/2 cups self-rising flour*
   1/2 cup baking cocoa
      1 cup chopped pecans
      1 jar (7 ounces) marshmallow creme
FROSTING:
   1/2 cup butter *or* margarine, softened
3-3/4 cups confectioners' sugar
      3 tablespoons baking cocoa
      1 tablespoon vanilla extract
      4 to 5 tablespoons milk
      1 cup chopped pecans

In a mixing bowl, cream butter and sugar. Add eggs, one at a time, beating well after each addition. Combine flour and cocoa; gradually add to creamed mixture. Fold in the pecans. Transfer to a greased 13-in. x 9-in. x 2-in. baking pan. Bake at 350° for 35-40 minutes or until a toothpick inserted near the center comes out clean.

Cool for 3 minutes (cake will fall in the center). Spoon the marshmallow creme over cake; carefully spread to cover top. Cool completely. For frosting, in a mixing bowl, cream butter. Beat in confectioners' sugar, cocoa, vanilla and enough milk to achieve frosting consistency. Fold in pecans. Spread over marshmallow creme layer. Store in the refrigerator. **Yield:** 16-20 servings.

*Editor's Note: As a substitute for each 1/2 cup of self-rising flour, place 3/4 teaspoon baking powder and 1/4 teaspoon salt in a 1/2-cup measuring cup. Add all-purpose flour to measure 1/2 cup.

Peanut Butter Chocolate Cake

Dorcas Yoder, Weyers Cave, Virginia

(Pictured above)

In our chocolate-loving house, this cake disappears very quickly! Cream cheese and peanut butter combine to create a finger-licking-good frosting.

        2 cups all-purpose flour
        2 cups sugar
    2/3 cup baking cocoa
        2 teaspoons baking soda
        1 teaspoon baking powder
    1/2 teaspoon salt
        2 eggs
        1 cup milk
    2/3 cup vegetable oil
        1 teaspoon vanilla extract
        1 cup brewed coffee, room temperature
PEANUT BUTTER FROSTING:
        1 package (3 ounces) cream cheese, softened
    1/4 cup creamy peanut butter
        2 cups confectioners' sugar
        2 tablespoons milk
    1/2 teaspoon vanilla extract
Miniature semisweet chocolate chips

In a mixing bowl, combine dry ingredients. Add eggs, milk, oil and vanilla; beat for 2 minutes. Stir in coffee (batter will be thin). Pour into a greased 13-in. x 9-in. x 2-in. baking pan. Bake at 350° for 35-40 minutes or until a toothpick inserted near the center comes out clean. Cool completely on a wire rack.

For frosting, beat the cream cheese and peanut butter in a mixing bowl until smooth. Beat in sugar, milk and vanilla. Spread over cake. Sprinkle with chocolate chips. Store in the refrigerator. **Yield:** 12-16 servings.

Root Beer Float Cake

Kat Thompson, Prineville, Oregon

I add root beer to both the cake batter and fluffy frosting of this summery dessert to get that great root beer float taste. Serve this moist cake to a bunch of hungry kids and watch it disappear.

        1 package (18-1/4 ounces) white cake mix
    1-3/4 cups cold root beer, *divided*
    1/4 cup vegetable oil
        2 eggs
        1 envelope whipped topping mix

In a mixing bowl, combine dry cake mix, 1-1/4 cups root beer, oil and eggs. Beat on low speed for 2 minutes or stir by hand for 3 minutes. Pour into a greased 13-in. x 9-in. x 2-in. baking pan. Bake at 350° for 30-35 minutes or until a toothpick inserted near the center comes out clean. Cool completely on a wire rack.

In a mixing bowl, combine whipped topping mix and remaining root beer. Beat until soft peaks form. Frost cake. Store in the refrigerator. **Yield:** 12-16 servings.

Pop-ular Alternatives

FOR A FUN and tasty variation, replace the root beer in the above cake with cherry, orange or another fruit-flavored soda.

Rhubarb Custard Cake

Evelyn Gebhardt, Kasilof, Alaska

Rhubarb thrives in my northern garden and is one of the few crops the pesky moose don't bother! Of all the rhubarb desserts I've tried, this pudding cake is my No. 1 choice. It has old-fashioned appeal but is so simple to prepare.

   1 package (18-1/4 ounces) yellow cake mix
   4 cups chopped fresh *or* frozen rhubarb
   1 cup sugar
   1 cup whipping cream
Whipped cream and fresh mint, optional

Prepare cake batter according to package directions. Pour into a greased 13-in. x 9-in. x 2-in. baking dish. Sprinkle with rhubarb and sugar. Slowly pour cream over top. Bake at 350° for 40-45 minutes or until golden brown. Cool for 15 minutes before serving. Garnish with whipped cream and mint if desired. Refrigerate leftovers. **Yield:** 12-15 servings.

Cream Cheese Sheet Cake

Gaye Mann, Washington, North Carolina

(Pictured below)

This tender buttery sheet cake with its fudgy chocolate glaze is a real crowd-pleaser. It's always popular at potlucks and parties. It's not uncommon to see folks going back for second and even third slices.

   **1 cup plus 2 tablespoons butter *or* margarine,
      softened**
   **2 packages (3 ounces *each*) cream cheese,
      softened**
2-1/4 cups sugar
   6 eggs
   3/4 teaspoon vanilla extract
2-1/4 cups cake flour

FROSTING:
   1 cup sugar
1/3 cup evaporated milk
1/2 cup butter *or* margarine
1/2 cup semisweet chocolate chips

In a mixing bowl, cream butter, cream cheese and sugar. Add eggs, one at a time, beating well after each addition. Beat in vanilla. Add flour; mix well. Pour into a greased 15-in. x 10-in. x 1-in. baking pan. Bake at 325° for 30-35 minutes or until a toothpick inserted near center comes out clean. Cool completely on a wire rack.

For frosting, combine sugar and milk in a saucepan; bring to a boil over medium heat. Cover and cook for 3 minutes (do not stir). Stir in butter and chocolate chips until melted. Cool slightly. Stir; spread over cake. **Yield:** 24-30 servings.

Sweet Potato Cake

Wanda Rolen, Sevierville, Tennessee

Just like my mom, I love to cook. I bake a lot for church dinners and homecomings, and many people have told me how much they like this cake.

   1 cup vegetable oil
   2 cups sugar
   4 eggs
**1-1/2 cups finely shredded uncooked sweet
      potato (about 1 medium)**
   1/4 cup hot water
   1 teaspoon vanilla extract
2-1/2 cups self-rising flour*
   1 teaspoon ground cinnamon
   1 cup sliced almonds
FROSTING:
   1/2 cup butter *or* margarine
   1 cup packed brown sugar
   1 cup evaporated milk
   3 egg yolks, beaten
1-1/2 cups flaked coconut
   1 cup sliced almonds
   1 teaspoon vanilla extract

In a mixing bowl, beat oil and sugar. Add eggs, one at a time, beating well after each addition. Add sweet potato, water and vanilla; mix well. Combine flour and cinnamon; add to potato mixture. Stir in almonds. Pour into a greased 13-in. x 9-in. x 2-in. baking pan. Bake at 350° for 40-45 minutes or until a toothpick inserted near the center comes out clean.

For frosting, melt butter in a saucepan; whisk in sugar, milk and egg yolks until smooth. Bring to a boil over medium heat; boil gently for 2 minutes. Remove from the heat; stir in coconut, almonds and vanilla. Spread over warm cake. Cool on a wire rack. **Yield:** 12-15 servings.

*Editor's Note: As a substitute for each 1/2 cup of self-rising flour, place 3/4 teaspoon baking powder and 1/4 teaspoon salt in a 1/2-cup measuring cup. Add all-purpose flour to measure 1/2 cup.

4 medium tart apples, peeled and chopped
   (4 cups)
1 cup chopped pecans
1 package (11 ounces) butterscotch chips

In a mixing bowl, beat the eggs, oil and vanilla. Combine flour, sugar, baking powder, salt, baking soda and cinnamon; add to egg mixture and mix well. Stir in apples and pecans.

Pour into an ungreased 13-in. x 9-in. x 2-in. baking dish. Sprinkle with chips. Bake at 325° for 40-45 minutes or until a toothpick inserted near the center comes out clean. Cool on a wire rack. **Yield:** 12-15 servings.

Crumb Cake

Kathy Lucas, Mechanicsburg, Pennsylvania

(Pictured above)

My favorite time to visit my grandmother was when she'd just taken her crumb cake out of the oven. A warm piece of that cake with a cold glass of milk was the best treat. I now make it often for my own family.

1/2 cup shortening
1 cup sugar
2 cups all-purpose flour
1 teaspoon baking soda
1/2 teaspoon salt
1 cup buttermilk
Confectioners' sugar

In a mixing bowl, cream shortening and sugar. Combine dry ingredients; add to creamed mixture alternately with buttermilk. Pour into a greased and floured 9-in. round baking pan. Bake at 375° for 35 minutes or until a toothpick inserted near the center comes out clean. Cool for 10 minutes; remove from pan to a wire rack to cool completely. Before serving, dust with confectioners' sugar. **Yield:** 8 servings.

Butterscotch Apple Cake

Beth Struble, Bryan, Ohio

My family often requests this easy old-fashioned cake for get-togethers—especially in the fall. The butterscotch and apple flavors blend fantastically.

3 eggs
1-1/4 cups vegetable oil
1 teaspoon vanilla extract
2-1/2 cups all-purpose flour
2 cups sugar
2 teaspoons baking powder
1 teaspoon salt
1 teaspoon baking soda
1 teaspoon ground cinnamon

Peanut Crunch Cake

Sue Smith, Norwalk, Connecticut

(Pictured below)

Here's a recipe that dresses up a plain box cake mix. Peanut butter and chocolate chips add fun, yummy flavor to this yellow cake.

1 package (18-1/4 ounces) yellow cake mix
1 cup peanut butter
1/2 cup packed brown sugar
1 cup water
3 eggs
1/4 cup vegetable oil
1/2 to 3/4 cup semisweet chocolate chips,
   divided
1/2 to 3/4 cup peanut butter chips, *divided*
1/2 cup chopped peanuts

In a mixing bowl, beat cake mix, peanut butter and brown sugar on low speed until crumbly. Set aside 1/2 cup. Add water, eggs and oil to remaining crumb mixture; blend on low until moistened. Beat on high for 2 minutes. Stir in 1/4 cup each chocolate and peanut butter chips. Pour into a greased 13-in. x 9-in. x 2-in. baking pan. Combine peanuts, reserved crumb mixture and the remaining chips; sprinkle over batter.

Bake at 350° for 40-45 minutes or until a toothpick inserted near the center comes out clean. Cool completely on a wire rack. **Yield:** 12-16 servings.

Old-Fashioned Carrot Cake

Muriel Doherty, Phoenix, Arizona

(Pictured below)

My family thinks this is the best carrot cake ever! We love the moist texture. The surprise is in the frosting. It's a pleasant departure from the usual cream cheese frosting that tops most carrot cakes. This cake doesn't last long around our house!

- 4 eggs
- 2 cups sugar
- 3 cups finely shredded carrots
- 1 package (8 ounces) cream cheese, softened
- 1-1/2 cups vegetable oil
- 2 cups all-purpose flour
- 2 teaspoons baking soda
- 2 teaspoons ground cinnamon
- 1 teaspoon salt
- 1 can (8 ounces) crushed pineapple, drained
- 1 cup chopped walnuts

FLUFFY FROSTING:
- 1/4 cup all-purpose flour
- 3/4 cup milk
- 3/4 cup butter *or* margarine, softened
- 3/4 cup sugar
- 1/2 teaspoon salt
- 1 teaspoon vanilla extract
- 2 cups confectioners' sugar

Additional chopped walnuts

Beat eggs and sugar. Add carrots, cream cheese and oil; beat until smooth. Add dry ingredients; mix well. Stir in pineapple and nuts. Pour into a greased 13-in. x 9-in. x 2-in. baking pan. Bake at 350° for 55-60 minutes or until a toothpick inserted near the center comes out clean. Cool completely on a wire rack.

In a heavy saucepan, cook and stir flour and milk over medium-low heat until a thick paste forms, about 10 minutes. Chill for 30 minutes. Cream butter, sugar and salt. Gradually add chilled flour mixture; beat until fluffy, about 5 minutes. Add vanilla and sugar; beat well. Frost cake. Sprinkle with nuts. Store in the refrigerator. **Yield:** 12-16 servings.

Elegant Chocolate Cake

Laura German, North Brookfield, Massachusetts

(Pictured above)

My mom fixed this chocolate cake for me when I came home from college. Now I serve it to my family. They love the yummy pecan-packed caramel sauce.

- 3 eggs
- 1 cup sugar
- 3/4 cup vegetable oil
- 1/4 cup milk
- 3/4 cup all-purpose flour
- 1/2 cup cocoa
- 1/2 teaspoon baking powder
- 1/2 teaspoon salt
- 1/2 teaspoon vanilla extract
- 1 package (14 ounces) caramels
- 1/4 cup water
- 1 cup chopped pecans

Whipped cream and additional chopped pecans, optional

In a mixing bowl, beat eggs, sugar, oil and milk. Combine the flour, cocoa, baking powder and salt; gradually add to egg mixture and mix well. Stir in vanilla. Transfer to a greased 8-in. square baking pan. Bake at 350° for 30-35 minutes or until a toothpick inserted near the center comes out clean. Cool on a wire rack.

In a heavy saucepan, combine caramels and water. Cook and stir over low heat until smooth. Add pecans. Cool slightly. Cut the cake into squares; drizzle with warm caramel sauce. Top with whipped cream and pecans if desired. **Yield:** 9 servings.

Banana Snack Cake

Dawn Fagerstrom, Warren, Minnesota

I often make this moist banana cake for birthdays. The recipe is good for making cupcakes, too—they taste great even without the frosting.

    1/2 cup shortening
    3/4 cup packed brown sugar
    1/2 cup sugar
      2 eggs
      1 cup mashed ripe bananas (2 to 3 medium)
      1 teaspoon vanilla extract
      2 cups all-purpose *or* whole wheat flour
      1 teaspoon baking soda
      1 teaspoon salt
    1/2 cup buttermilk
    1/2 cup chopped nuts
FROSTING (optional):
    1/2 cup packed brown sugar
    1/4 cup butter *or* margarine
      6 tablespoons milk
2-1/2 to 3 cups confectioners' sugar

In a mixing bowl, cream shortening and sugars. Add eggs, one at a time, beating well after each addition. Beat in bananas and vanilla. Combine flour, baking soda and salt; add to the creamed mixture alternately with buttermilk. Stir in nuts. Pour into a greased 13-in. x 9-in. x 2-in. baking pan. Bake at 350° for 25-30 minutes or until a toothpick inserted near the center comes out clean. Cool completely on a wire rack.

For frosting, combine brown sugar, butter and milk in a saucepan. Bring to a boil over medium heat; boil and stir for 2 minutes. Remove from the heat; cool to lukewarm. Gradually beat in confectioners' sugar until frosting reaches spreading consistency. Frost the cake. **Yield:** 12 servings.

Grandma's Blackberry Cake

Diana Martin, Moundsville, West Virginia

I remember going blackberry picking with Mom and Grandma. Even at 70 years old, Grandma could pick 3 gallons of berries before I had my pail half full. Grandma made up this recipe with her mom, and it's been passed down for five generations now.

      1 cup fresh blackberries
      2 cups all-purpose flour, *divided*
    1/2 cup butter *or* margarine, softened
      1 cup sugar
      2 eggs
      1 teaspoon baking soda
      1 teaspoon ground cinnamon
      1 teaspoon ground nutmeg
    1/2 teaspoon salt
    1/4 teaspoon ground cloves
    1/4 teaspoon ground allspice
    3/4 cup buttermilk
Whipped cream, optional

Toss blackberries with 2 tablespoons of flour; set aside. In a mixing bowl, cream butter and sugar. Add eggs; beat well. Combine baking soda, cinnamon, nutmeg, salt, cloves, allspice and remaining flour; add to creamed mixture alternately with buttermilk. Fold in blackberries. Pour into a greased 9-in. square baking pan.

Bake at 350° for 45-50 minutes or until a toothpick inserted near the center comes out clean. Cool completely on a wire rack. Serve with whipped cream if desired. **Yield:** 9 servings.

Glazed Lemon Cake

Missy Andrews, Rice, Washington

(Pictured below)

My mother baked this light moist treat when I was a child. I loved it as much then as my children do now. Boxed cake and pudding mixes make this delightful dessert simple to make.

      1 package (18-1/4 ounces) white cake mix
      1 package (3.4 ounces) instant lemon pudding mix
    3/4 cup vegetable oil
      3 eggs
      1 cup lemon-lime soda
      1 cup confectioners' sugar
      2 tablespoons lemon juice

In a mixing bowl, combine the cake mix, pudding mix, oil and eggs; beat on medium speed for 1 minute. Gradually beat in soda. Pour into a greased 13-in. x 9-in. x 2-in. baking dish. Bake at 350° for 40-45 minutes or until cake springs back when lightly touched in center.

Combine confectioners' sugar and lemon juice until smooth; carefully spread over warm cake. Cool on a wire rack. **Yield:** 12 servings.

White Chocolate Fudge Cake

Denise Heydinger, Shelby, Ohio

(Pictured below)

This cake, with its thick frosting and rich chocolate layer, is a big hit at office potlucks. One co-worker tells everyone it's awful so he can have it all to himself!

1 package (18-1/4 ounces) white cake mix
1-1/4 cups water
3 egg whites
1/3 cup vegetable oil
1 teaspoon vanilla extract
3 squares (1 ounce *each*) white baking chocolate, melted

FILLING:
3/4 cup semisweet chocolate chips
2 tablespoons butter (no substitutes)

FROSTING:
1 can (16 ounces) vanilla frosting
3 squares (1 ounce *each*) white baking chocolate, melted
1 teaspoon vanilla extract
1 carton (8 ounces) frozen whipped topping, thawed

In a mixing bowl, combine the dry cake mix, water, egg whites, oil and vanilla. Beat on low for 2 minutes. Stir in white chocolate. Pour into a greased 13-in. x 9-in. x 2-in. baking pan. Bake at 350° for 25-30 minutes or until a toothpick inserted near the center comes out clean. Cool for 5 minutes.

Meanwhile, in a microwave or heavy saucepan over low heat, melt chocolate chips and butter; stir until smooth. Carefully spread over warm cake. Cool completely. In a mixing bowl, beat frosting; stir in white chocolate and vanilla. Fold in whipped topping; frost cake. Store in the refrigerator. **Yield:** 16 servings.

Hawaiian Cake

Jo Ann Fox, Johnson City, Tennessee

Widely known as a symbol of hospitality, pineapple inspired a theme dinner my husband and I hosted a few years ago. Pairing pineapple with coconut lent a tropical flavor to the dessert served as the finale to our party. This recipe has been in my file for over 20 years and never fails to delight.

1 package (18-1/4 ounces) yellow cake mix
1-1/4 cups cold milk
1 package (3.4 ounces) instant vanilla pudding mix
1 can (20 ounces) crushed pineapple, drained
1 envelope whipped topping mix
1 package (3 ounces) cream cheese, softened
1/4 cup sugar
1/2 teaspoon vanilla extract
1/2 cup flaked coconut, toasted

Prepare and bake the cake according to package directions, using a greased 13-in. x 9-in. x 2-in. baking pan. Cool completely on a wire rack. In a bowl, whisk together milk and pudding mix; let stand to thicken. Stir in pineapple. Spread over cake. Prepare whipped topping mix according to package directions; set aside.

In a mixing bowl, beat cream cheese, sugar and vanilla until smooth. Beat in 1 cup whipped topping. Fold in remaining topping. Spread over pudding. Sprinkle with coconut. Cover and refrigerate for 3 hours or overnight. **Yield:** 12-15 servings.

Gingerbread with Brown Sugar Sauce

Toni Hamm, Vandergrift, Pennsylvania

(Pictured above)

The aroma of gingerbread baking in the oven is what I remember most about my grandmother's kitchen, and it meant dessert would be special. That was nearly 50 years ago, but whenever I catch a whiff of ginger and cinnamon, I'm back with Grandmother and the happiness I knew.

> 6 tablespoons shortening
> 1/2 cup packed brown sugar
> 1/3 cup molasses
> 1 egg
> 1-1/2 cups all-purpose flour
> 1/2 teaspoon baking soda
> 1/2 teaspoon ground cinnamon
> 1/2 teaspoon ground ginger
> 1/8 teaspoon salt
> 1/2 cup buttermilk
> **BROWN SUGAR SAUCE:**
> 1 cup packed brown sugar
> 4-1/2 teaspoons cornstarch
> 1/2 cup cold water
> 1-1/2 teaspoons vinegar
> 1 tablespoon butter *or* margarine
> 1-1/2 teaspoons vanilla extract

In a mixing bowl, cream shortening, brown sugar, molasses and egg; mix well. Combine flour, baking soda, cinnamon, ginger and salt; add to the molasses mixture alternately with buttermilk. Pour into a greased and floured 9-in. round baking pan. Bake at 350° for 25-30 minutes or until a toothpick inserted near the center comes out clean. Cool for 10 minutes before removing from pan to a wire rack.

For sauce, combine brown sugar, cornstarch, water and vinegar in a saucepan; stir until smooth. Add butter. Bring to a boil; boil and stir for 2 minutes. Remove from the heat and stir in vanilla. Serve over the gingerbread. **Yield:** 6-8 servings.

Pumpkin Sheet Cake

Nancy Baker, Boonville, Missouri

(Pictured below)

The pastor at our church usually cuts his sermon short on carry-in dinner days because he knows this sheet cake is waiting in the fellowship hall. This moist cake travels well and is also easy to prepare.

> 1 can (15 ounces) pumpkin
> 2 cups sugar
> 1 cup vegetable oil
> 4 eggs, lightly beaten
> 2 cups all-purpose flour
> 2 teaspoons baking soda
> 1 teaspoon ground cinnamon
> 1/2 teaspoon salt
> **FROSTING:**
> 1 package (3 ounces) cream cheese, softened
> 5 tablespoons butter *or* margarine, softened
> 1 teaspoon vanilla extract
> 1-3/4 cups confectioners' sugar
> 3 to 4 teaspoons milk
> **Chopped nuts**

In a mixing bowl, beat pumpkin, sugar and oil. Add eggs; mix well. Combine flour, baking soda, cinnamon and salt; add to pumpkin mixture and beat until well blended. Pour into a greased 15-in. x 10-in. x 1-in. baking pan. Bake at 350° for 25-30 minutes or until a toothpick inserted near the center comes out clean. Cool completely on a wire rack.

For frosting, beat the cream cheese, butter and vanilla in a mixing bowl until smooth. Gradually add sugar; mix well. Add milk until frosting reaches desired spreading consistency. Frost cake. Sprinkle with nuts. **Yield:** 20-24 servings.

German Chocolate Birthday Cake

Lisa Andis, Morristown, Indiana

(Pictured above)

This moist, flavorful cake was the traditional birthday cake at our house when I was growing up. Everyone requested it. I especially like the sweet coconut-pecan frosting.

      1 package (4 ounces) German sweet
         chocolate
   1/2 cup water
      1 cup butter *or* margarine, softened
      2 cups sugar
      4 eggs, *separated*
      1 teaspoon vanilla extract
2-1/2 cups cake flour
      1 teaspoon baking soda
   1/2 teaspoon salt
      1 cup buttermilk
COCONUT-PECAN FROSTING:
      1 cup evaporated milk
      1 cup sugar
      3 egg yolks, lightly beaten
   1/2 cup butter *or* margarine
      1 teaspoon vanilla extract
1-1/3 cups flaked coconut
      1 cup chopped pecans

In a saucepan over low heat, stir chocolate and water until chocolate is melted. Cool. In a mixing bowl, cream butter and sugar. Add egg yolks, one at a time, beating well after each addition. Add chocolate mixture and vanilla; mix well. Combine flour, baking soda and salt; add alternately with buttermilk to creamed mixture. In another mixing bowl, beat egg whites until stiff peaks form; fold into batter. Line a greased 13-in. x 9-in. x 2-in. baking pan with waxed paper. Grease and flour the

paper. Spread batter evenly in pan. Bake at 350° for 50-55 minutes or until a toothpick inserted near the center comes out clean. Cool in pan for 10 minutes; invert onto a wire rack to cool completely. Remove waxed paper.

For frosting, combine milk, sugar, egg yolks, butter and vanilla in a saucepan; cook and stir over medium heat until thickened. Remove from the heat; stir in coconut and pecans. Beat until frosting is cool and reaches desired spreading consistency. Place cake on a serving platter; spread frosting over top and sides. **Yield:** 12-15 servings.

Coconut Poppy Seed Cake

Gail Cayce, Wautoma, Wisconsin

(Pictured below)

This moist coconut cake is definitely one of my most-requested desserts. Use different cake mixes and pudding flavors for variety.

      1 package (18-1/4 ounces) white cake mix
   1/4 cup poppy seeds
   1/4 teaspoon coconut extract, optional
3-1/2 cups cold milk
      2 packages (3.4 ounces *each*) instant coconut
         cream pudding mix
      1 carton (8 ounces) frozen whipped topping,
         thawed
   1/3 cup flaked coconut, toasted, optional

Prepare cake according to package directions, adding poppy seeds and coconut extract if desired to batter. Pour into a greased 13-in. x 9-in. x 2-in. baking pan. Bake at 350° for 20-25 minutes or until a toothpick inserted near the center comes out clean. Cool completely on a wire rack.

In a mixing bowl, beat milk and pudding mix on low speed for 2 minutes. Spread over the cake. Spread with whipped topping. Sprinkle with coconut if desired. **Yield:** 20-24 servings.

Upside-Down Raspberry Cake

Joy Beck, Cincinnati, Ohio

This moist cake is great for any occasion. Pretty red berries peek out of every slice. I've received many compliments from family and friends and I'm always asked for a copy of the recipe.

1-1/2 cups fresh *or* frozen unsweetened
    raspberries, *divided
1 cup butter *or* margarine, softened
1 cup sugar
3 eggs
2 teaspoons lemon juice
1 teaspoon vanilla extract
2 cups all-purpose flour
1-1/2 teaspoons baking powder
1/2 teaspoon salt
2/3 cup milk
Confectioners' sugar

Line the bottom and sides of a 9-in. square baking pan with foil; coat with nonstick cooking spray. Place 1/2 cup raspberries in pan; set aside. In a mixing bowl, cream butter and sugar. Add eggs, lemon juice and vanilla; mix well. Combine flour, baking powder and salt; add to creamed mixture alternately with milk.

Fold in the remaining raspberries. Carefully spoon over berries in pan. Bake at 350° for 40-45 minutes or until a toothpick inserted near the center comes out clean. Cool for 10 minutes. Invert cake onto a serving platter; carefully remove foil. Cool completely. Dust with confectioners' sugar. **Yield:** 9 servings.

*Editor's Note: If using frozen raspberries, do not thaw before adding to batter.

Cream Cake Dessert

Peggy Stott, Burlington, Iowa

(Pictured above right)

Folks of all ages really go for this light yellow cake with fluffy cream filling in the middle. My son first tried this treat while in high school and asked me to get the recipe. I've used it countless times since for all sorts of occasions. It's easy to transport to a potluck because the cream is on the inside.

1 package (18-1/4 ounces) yellow cake mix
1 package (3.4 ounces) instant vanilla
    pudding mix
1/2 cup shortening
1 cup water
4 eggs
FILLING:
5 tablespoons all-purpose flour
1 cup milk
1/2 cup butter *or* margarine, softened
1/2 cup shortening
1 cup sugar
1 teaspoon vanilla extract
1/2 teaspoon salt
Fresh raspberries, optional

In a mixing bowl, beat cake mix, pudding mix and shortening on low speed until crumbly. Add the water and eggs; beat on medium for 2 minutes. Pour into a greased and floured 13-in. x 9-in. x 2-in. baking pan. Bake at 350° for 30-35 minutes or until a toothpick inserted near the center comes out clean. Cool for 10 minutes; invert onto a wire rack to cool completely.

Meanwhile, in a saucepan, combine the flour and milk until smooth. Bring to a boil; cook and stir for 2 minutes or until thickened. Cool completely. In a mixing bowl, cream the butter, shortening, sugar, vanilla and salt; beat in the milk mixture until the sugar is dissolved, about 5 minutes.

Split cake into two horizontal layers. Spread filling over the bottom layer; replace top layer. Cut into serving-size pieces. Garnish with raspberries if desired. **Yield:** 16-20 servings.

Flour Power

FOR THE BEST results, do not substitute cake flour if a recipe calls for all-purpose flour and vice versa. They are not interchangeable.

Store flour in airtight containers, such as canisters, at room temperature for up to 6 months.

Pumpkin Orange Cake

Shirley Glaab, Hattiesburg, Mississippi

(Pictured below)

This moist make-ahead spice cake with its flavorful orange frosting is popular at family gatherings. It's simple to prepare and it tastes so good, everyone asks for the recipe.

- 1/2 cup butter *or* margarine, softened
- 1-1/4 cups sugar
- 2 eggs
- 1 cup cooked *or* canned pumpkin
- 1/2 cup orange juice
- 1/4 cup milk
- 1 tablespoon grated orange peel
- 2 cups all-purpose flour
- 3 teaspoons baking powder
- 1 teaspoon ground cinnamon
- 1/2 teaspoon baking soda
- 1/2 teaspoon salt
- 1/2 teaspoon ground ginger
- 1/2 teaspoon ground allspice
- 1/2 cup chopped walnuts

ORANGE FROSTING:
- 1/3 cup butter *or* margarine, softened
- 3 cups confectioners' sugar
- 3 tablespoons milk
- 2 teaspoons orange juice
- 4-1/2 teaspoons grated orange peel

In a mixing bowl, cream butter and sugar. Add eggs, one at a time, beating well after each addition. In another mixing bowl, beat pumpkin, orange juice, milk and orange peel. Combine dry ingredients; add to creamed mixture alternately with pumpkin mixture. Fold in nuts.

Pour into a greased 13-in. x 9-in. x 2-in. baking pan. Bake at 350° for 30 minutes or until a toothpick inserted near the center comes out clean. Cool on a wire rack.

For frosting, combine butter and confectioners' sugar in a mixing bowl. Beat in the milk, orange juice and peel. Frost cake. **Yield:** 12 servings.

Lazy Daisy Cake

Darlis Wilfer, Phelps, Wisconsin

(Pictured above)

We couldn't wait until Mom sliced this old-fashioned cake with its caramel-like frosting, loaded with chewy coconut. Even after one of Mom's delicious meals, one piece of this cake wasn't enough.

- 4 eggs
- 2 cups sugar
- 2 teaspoons vanilla extract
- 2 cups all-purpose flour
- 2 teaspoons baking powder
- 1/2 teaspoon salt
- 1 cup milk
- 1/4 cup butter *or* margarine

FROSTING:
- 1-1/2 cups packed brown sugar
- 3/4 cup butter *or* margarine, melted
- 1/2 cup half-and-half cream
- 2 cups flaked coconut

In a mixing bowl, beat eggs, sugar and vanilla until thick, about 4 minutes. Combine flour, baking powder and salt; add to egg mixture and beat just until combined. In a saucepan, bring milk and butter to a boil, stirring constantly. Add to batter; beat until combined.

Pour into a greased 13-in. x 9-in. x 2-in. baking pan. Bake at 350° for 35-40 minutes or until a toothpick inserted near the center comes out clean. Combine frosting ingredients; spread over warm cake. Broil until lightly browned, about 3-4 minutes. **Yield:** 16-20 servings.

Microwave Oatmeal Cake

Ruby Williams, Bogalusa, Louisiana

This cake is a yummy treat with a scrumptious topping. It's a snap to make.

- 1 cup quick-cooking oats
- 1-1/2 cups water

        1/2 cup butter *or* margarine, softened
            1 cup packed brown sugar
        1/2 cup sugar
            2 eggs
    1-1/2 teaspoons vanilla extract
    1-1/3 cups all-purpose flour
            1 teaspoon baking soda
            1 teaspoon ground cinnamon
        1/2 teaspoon salt
        1/4 teaspoon ground nutmeg
TOPPING:
            1 cup flaked coconut
        1/2 cup chopped nuts
        1/2 cup packed brown sugar
        1/2 cup milk
        1/4 cup butter *or* margarine

In a microwave-safe bowl, combine oats and water. Microwave, uncovered, on high for 2-3 minutes or until thickened, stirring once; set aside. In a mixing bowl, cream butter and sugars. Add eggs; beat well. Beat in vanilla and oat mixture. Combine dry ingredients; gradually add to oat mixture and mix well. Pour into a greased 11-in. x 7-in. x 2-in. microwave-safe dish. Shield corners with small triangles of foil.*

Microwave, uncovered, at 50% power for 8 minutes. Cook on high for 6 minutes or until when center is touched, cake clings to finger while area underneath is almost dry. Place on a wire rack. Combine topping ingredients in a microwave-safe dish; heat, uncovered, on high for 6-7 minutes or until thick and bubbly, stirring every 2 minutes. Spread over warm cake. **Yield:** 8 servings.

*Editor's Note: Shielding with small pieces of foil prevents overcooking of food in the corners of a square or rectangular dish. Secure foil firmly to dish and do not allow it to touch insides of microwave. This recipe was tested in an 850-watt microwave.

Cranberry Cake
Marion Lowery, Medford, Oregon
(Pictured below)

This traditional pudding-like dessert is my mother's recipe. It's always welcomed on holidays. The moist, colorful cake is served with a rich, buttery sauce.

        3 tablespoons butter (no substitutes),
            softened
            1 cup sugar
            1 egg
            2 cups all-purpose flour
            2 teaspoons baking powder
            1 teaspoon ground nutmeg
            1 cup milk
            2 cups cranberries
            2 tablespoons grated orange *or* lemon peel
CREAM SAUCE:
    1-1/3 cups sugar
            1 cup whipping cream
        2/3 cup butter

In a mixing bowl, cream butter and sugar. Beat in egg. Combine the flour, baking powder and nutmeg; add to the creamed mixture alternately with milk. Stir in cranberries and orange peel.

Pour into a greased 11-in. x 7-in. x 2-in. baking dish. Bake at 350° for 35-40 minutes or until a toothpick inserted near the center comes out clean. Meanwhile, in a saucepan, combine sauce ingredients. Cook and stir over medium heat until heated through. Cut warm cake into squares; serve with cream sauce. **Yield:** 8-10 servings.

Walnut Apple Cake

Jacquelyn Remsberg, La Canada, California

(Pictured above)

I first tasted this delicious cake at a Halloween party and quickly asked for the recipe. It's not too sweet, and the butter sauce makes it a super dessert.

   2 eggs
   2 cups sugar
1/2 cup vegetable oil
   2 teaspoons vanilla extract
   2 cups all-purpose flour
2-1/2 teaspoons ground cinnamon
   2 teaspoons baking soda
   1 teaspoon salt
1/4 teaspoon ground nutmeg
   4 cups chopped peeled tart apples
   1 cup chopped walnuts
BUTTER SAUCE:
 3/4 cup sugar
   3 tablespoons all-purpose flour
   1 cup milk
   2 tablespoons butter (no substitutes)
   1 teaspoon vanilla extract
Walnut halves, optional

In a mixing bowl, combine eggs, sugar, oil and vanilla; mix well. Combine dry ingredients; add to the egg mixture and mix well (batter will be stiff). Stir in apples and walnuts. Spread into a greased 13-in. x 9-in. x 2-in. baking pan. Bake at 350° for 45-50 minutes or until a toothpick inserted near the center comes out clean. Cool completely on a wire rack.

For sauce, combine sugar, flour, milk and butter in a saucepan. Bring to a boil over medium heat; boil and stir for 2 minutes. Remove from heat; stir in vanilla. Cut cake into squares; top with warm sauce. Garnish with walnut halves if desired. **Yield:** 12-15 servings.

Rich Butter Cake

Doris Schloeman, Naperville, Illinois

I've been bringing this cake to family get-togethers since the 1950s. The scrumptious standby, topped with cream cheese and nuts, can be prepared in a wink.

   1 package (16 ounces) pound cake mix
1/2 cup butter *or* margarine, melted
   5 eggs
   2 cups confectioners' sugar, *divided*
   2 packages (one 8 ounces, one 3 ounces)
     cream cheese, softened
1/2 teaspoon vanilla extract
   1 cup chopped walnuts

In a large mixing bowl, combine the dry cake mix, butter and 3 eggs; beat until smooth. Spread into a greased 13-in. x 9-in. x 2-in. baking pan. Set aside 2 tablespoons confectioners' sugar for topping. In a bowl, beat the cream cheese, vanilla, remaining confectioners' sugar and remaining eggs. Pour over the batter. Sprinkle with walnuts.

Bake at 350° for 35-40 minutes or until cake begins to pull away from sides of pan. Cool on a wire rack. Dust with reserved confectioners' sugar. Store in the refrigerator. **Yield:** 12-15 servings.

White Texas Sheet Cake

Joanie Ward, Brownsburg, Indiana

(Pictured below)

This cake has creamy frosting and light almond flavor. No one can stop at just one piece.

   1 cup butter *or* margarine
   1 cup water
   2 cups all-purpose flour
   2 cups sugar
   2 eggs, beaten

1/2 cup sour cream
1 teaspoon almond extract
1 teaspoon salt
1 teaspoon baking soda
FROSTING:
1/2 cup butter *or* margarine
1/4 cup milk
4-1/2 cups confectioners' sugar
1/2 teaspoon almond extract
1 cup chopped walnuts

In a large saucepan, bring butter and water to a boil. Remove from the heat; stir in flour, sugar, eggs, sour cream, almond extract, salt and baking soda until smooth. Pour into a greased 15-in. x 10-in. x 1-in. baking pan. Bake at 375° for 20-22 minutes or until cake is golden brown and a toothpick inserted near the center comes out clean. Cool for 20 minutes.

Meanwhile, for frosting, combine butter and milk in a saucepan. Bring to a boil. Remove from the heat; add sugar and extract and mix well. Stir in walnuts; spread over warm cake. **Yield:** 16-20 servings.

Special Rhubarb Cake

Biena Schlabach, Millersburg, Ohio

A rich vanilla sauce is served with this tender cake. The women at church made it for my 84th birthday.

2 tablespoons butter (no substitutes), softened
1 cup sugar
1 egg
2 cups all-purpose flour
1 teaspoon baking powder
1/2 teaspoon baking soda
1/2 teaspoon salt
1 cup buttermilk
2 cups chopped fresh *or* frozen rhubarb, thawed
STREUSEL TOPPING:
1/4 cup all-purpose flour
1/4 cup sugar
2 tablespoons butter, melted
VANILLA SAUCE:
1/2 cup butter
3/4 cup sugar
1/2 cup evaporated milk
1 teaspoon vanilla extract

In a mixing bowl, cream butter and sugar. Beat in egg. Combine flour, baking powder, baking soda and salt; add to creamed mixture alternately with buttermilk, beating just until moistened. Fold in the rhubarb. Pour into a greased 9-in. square baking dish.

Combine topping ingredients; sprinkle over batter. Bake at 350° for 40-45 minutes or until a toothpick comes out clean. Cool on a wire rack.

For sauce, melt butter in a saucepan. Add sugar and milk. Bring to a boil; cook and stir for 2-3 minutes or until thickened. Remove from the heat; stir in vanilla. Serve with cake. **Yield:** 9 servings (1-1/4 cups sauce).

Upside-Down Strawberry Shortcake

Debra Falkiner, St. Charles, Missouri

(Pictured above)

For a tasty twist at dessert time, this shortcake has a bountiful berry layer on the bottom. It's a treat our family has savored for years.

1 cup miniature marshmallows
1 package (16 ounces) frozen sweetened sliced strawberries, thawed
1 package (3 ounces) strawberry gelatin
1/2 cup shortening
1-1/2 cups sugar
3 eggs
1 teaspoon vanilla extract
2-1/4 cups all-purpose flour
3 teaspoons baking powder
1/2 teaspoon salt
1 cup milk
Fresh strawberries and whipped cream

Sprinkle marshmallows evenly into a greased 13-in. x 9-in. x 2-in. baking dish; set aside. In a bowl, combine strawberries and gelatin powder; set aside. In a mixing bowl, cream shortening and sugar. Add the eggs, one at a time, beating well after each addition. Beat in vanilla. Combine flour, baking powder and salt; add to creamed mixture alternately with milk.

Pour batter over the marshmallows. Spoon strawberry mixture evenly over batter. Bake at 350° for 45-50 minutes or until a toothpick inserted near the center comes out clean. Cool on a wire rack. Cut into squares. Garnish with strawberries and whipped cream. **Yield:** 12-16 servings.

Chocolate Creme Cakes

Faith Sommers, Beckwourth, California

(Pictured above and on page 4)

Moist layers of chocolate cake sandwich a sweet and creamy filling in this irresistible recipe. The yummy treats are handy to keep in the freezer.

>   1 package (18-1/4 ounces) chocolate cake mix
>   1 package (3.9 ounces) instant chocolate
>   pudding mix
> 3/4 cup vegetable oil
> 3/4 cup water
>   4 eggs
> **FILLING:**
>   3 tablespoons all-purpose flour
>   1 cup milk
> 1/2 cup butter *or* margarine, softened
> 1/2 cup shortening
>   1 cup sugar
>   1 teaspoon vanilla extract

In a mixing bowl, combine cake and pudding mixes, oil, water and eggs; mix well. Pour into a greased and floured 13-in. x 9-in. x 2-in. baking pan. Bake at 350° for 30-35 minutes or until a toothpick inserted near the center comes out clean. Cool for 10 minutes; invert onto a wire rack to cool completely.

In a small saucepan, combine flour and milk until smooth. Bring to a boil; cook and stir for 2 minutes or until thickened. Cool. In a mixing bowl, cream the butter, shortening, sugar and vanilla; beat in milk mixture until

sugar is dissolved, about 5 minutes. Split cake into two horizontal layers. Spread filling over the bottom layer; cover with top layer. Cut into serving-size pieces. Freeze in an airtight container for up to 1 month. Remove from the freezer 1 hour before serving. **Yield:** 12-18 servings.

Raspberry Cake

Marion Anderson, Dalton, Minnesota

I jazz up a plain cake with raspberry gelatin and frozen berries. Spread with a light, fruity whipped topping, the festive results make a cool and refreshing dessert.

>   1 package (18-1/4 ounces) white cake mix
>   1 package (3 ounces) raspberry gelatin
>   1 package (10 ounces) frozen sweetened
>   raspberries, thawed, undrained
>   4 eggs
> 1/2 cup vegetable oil
> 1/4 cup hot water
> **FROSTING:**
>   1 carton (12 ounces) frozen whipped topping,
>   thawed
>   1 package (10 ounces) frozen sweetened
>   raspberries, thawed, undrained

In a large bowl, combine the dry cake mix and gelatin powder. Add the raspberries with juice, eggs, oil and water. Beat until well blended. Pour into a greased 13-

in. x 9-in. x 2-in. baking pan. Bake at 350° for 35-40 minutes or until a toothpick inserted near the center comes out clean. Cool on a wire rack.

For frosting, fold whipped topping into raspberries. Spread over cake. Refrigerate for 2 hours before serving. Store in the refrigerator. **Yield:** 12-16 servings.

Dinette Cake

Margaret Sanders, Indianapolis, Indiana

(Pictured below)

It takes only minutes to get this cake into the oven. It's one of my favorite desserts. I love serving this treat to guests, and it's one my grandchildren frequently ask me to make for them.

1-1/2 cups all-purpose flour
  1 cup sugar
  2 teaspoons baking powder
  1/2 teaspoon salt
  2/3 cup milk
  1/3 cup vegetable oil
  1 egg
  1 teaspoon vanilla extract
Fresh fruit *or* ice cream, optional

In a mixing bowl, combine flour, sugar, baking powder and salt. Add milk, oil, egg and vanilla; beat for 1 minute. Pour into a greased 9-in. square baking pan. Bake at 350° for 30-35 minutes or until a toothpick inserted near the center comes out clean. Cool on a wire rack. Serve with fruit or ice cream if desired. **Yield:** 8-9 servings.

Orange Blossom Cake

Mrs. E.W. Mueller, Mariposa, California

(Pictured above)

What could better represent our area than a recipe calling for oranges fresh off the tree? Since we planted and maintained a grove of 250 orange trees for almost 20 years, this recipe became a family favorite. Our grown children have said this cake brings back wonderful childhood memories.

  1/2 cup butter *or* margarine, softened
  1 cup sugar
  1/2 cup applesauce
  2 eggs
  1 tablespoon grated orange peel
2-1/2 cups all-purpose flour
  1 teaspoon baking powder
  1 teaspoon baking soda
  1/4 teaspoon salt
  1 cup buttermilk
  1 cup chopped dates
  1 cup chopped nuts
GLAZE:
  1 cup sugar
  1/2 cup orange juice

In a mixing bowl, cream butter and sugar. Add applesauce, eggs and orange peel; mix well. Combine the flour, baking powder, baking soda and salt. Add to creamed mixture alternately with milk; mix well. Fold in dates and nuts. Pour into a greased 9-in. springform pan. Bake at 350° for 55-60 minutes or until a toothpick inserted near the center comes out clean.

Meanwhile, combine glaze ingredients in a saucepan; bring to a boil. Pour over cake. Cool completely in pan. **Yield:** 10-12 servings.

Fast Fruit Cocktail Cake

Karen Naramore, Gillette, Wyoming

A convenient can of fruit cocktail is the key to this moist, down-home dessert. It's so comforting served warm with whipped cream or ice cream.

>   1 cup all-purpose flour
>   1 cup sugar
>   1 teaspoon baking soda
>   1 teaspoon salt
>   1 can (15-1/4 ounces) fruit cocktail, undrained
>   1 egg, beaten
> 1/2 cup packed brown sugar
> 1/2 cup chopped walnuts
> Whipped cream, optional

In a large bowl, combine the first six ingredients; stir until smooth. Pour into a greased 9-in. square baking pan. Combine brown sugar and nuts; sprinkle over top. Bake at 350° for 30-35 minutes or until a toothpick inserted near the center comes out clean. Serve with whipped cream if desired. **Yield:** 9 servings.

Orange Cream Cake

Star Pooley, Paradise, California

(Pictured above and on page 4)

Kids of all ages will enjoy the old-fashioned flavor of this super-moist cake topped with a soft light frosting. This dessert reminds me of the frozen Creamsicles I enjoyed as a child.

>   1 package (18-1/4 ounces) lemon cake mix
>   1 envelope unsweetened orange soft drink
>   mix
>   3 eggs
>   1 cup water
> 1/3 cup vegetable oil
>   2 packages (3 ounces *each*) orange gelatin,
>   *divided*
>   1 cup boiling water
>   1 cup cold water
>   1 cup cold milk
>   1 teaspoon vanilla extract
>   1 package (3.4 ounces) instant vanilla pudding
>   mix
>   1 carton (8 ounces) frozen whipped topping,
>   thawed

In a mixing bowl, combine cake and drink mixes, eggs, water and oil. Beat on medium speed for 2 minutes. Pour into an ungreased 13-in. x 9-in. x 2-in. baking pan. Bake at 350° for 25-30 minutes or until a toothpick inserted near the center comes out clean. Using a meat fork, poke holes in cake. Cool on a wire rack for 30 minutes.

Meanwhile, in a bowl, dissolve one package of gelatin in boiling water. Stir in cold water. Pour over cake. Cover and refrigerate for 2 hours. In a mixing bowl, combine milk, vanilla, pudding mix and remaining gelatin; beat on low for 2 minutes. Let stand for 5 minutes; fold in whipped topping. Frost cake. Refrigerate leftovers. **Yield:** 12-15 servings.

Praline Ice Cream Cake

Joan Hallford, North Richland Hills, Texas

(Pictured below and on page 4)

Melted ice cream is a key ingredient in this delectable golden cake. It's been a family favorite for years—we love the pecan praline flavor. It's also a joy to serve to company, since it's not tricky to fix and always wins rave reviews!

>   1 cup packed brown sugar
> 1/2 cup sour cream
>   2 tablespoons plus 1/2 cup butter *or*
>   margarine, *divided*

2 teaspoons cornstarch
1 teaspoon vanilla extract, *divided*
2 cups vanilla ice cream, softened
2 eggs
1-1/2 cups all-purpose flour
1 cup graham cracker crumbs (about 16 squares)
2/3 cup sugar
2-1/2 teaspoons baking powder
1/2 teaspoon salt
1/2 cup chopped pecans, toasted
Whipped cream, optional

In a heavy saucepan, combine the brown sugar, sour cream, 2 tablespoons butter and cornstarch. Cook and stir over medium heat until mixture comes to a boil. Remove from the heat. Stir in 1/2 teaspoon of vanilla; set aside.

Melt the remaining butter; place in a mixing bowl. Add ice cream; stir to blend. Add eggs, one at a time, beating well after each addition; stir in the remaining vanilla. Combine the flour, cracker crumbs, sugar, baking powder and salt; gradually add to ice cream mixture until combined. Pour into a greased 13-in. x 9-in. x 2-in. baking pan. Drizzle with half of the praline sauce.

Bake at 350° for 25-30 minutes or until a toothpick inserted near the center comes out clean. Cool on a wire rack. Add pecans to remaining sauce; spoon over warm cake (sauce will not cover the entire cake top). Cool in pan. Serve with whipped cream if desired. **Yield:** 15 servings.

Peach Cake

Donna Britsch, Tega Cay, South Carolina

I first tasted this cake about 15 years ago when a dear aunt brought it to a family reunion. I knew I had to have the recipe, and I was thrilled to discover how easy it is to make. Sometimes I'll scoop softened vanilla ice cream on each serving instead of spreading whipped topping over the entire cake.

3/4 cup cold butter *or* margarine
1 package (18-1/2 ounces) yellow cake mix
2 egg yolks
2 cups (16 ounces) sour cream
1 can (29 ounces) sliced peaches, drained
1/2 teaspoon ground cinnamon
1 carton (8 ounces) frozen whipped topping, thawed

In a bowl, cut butter into dry cake mix until the mixture resembles coarse crumbs. Pat into a greased 13-in. x 9-in. x 2-in. baking pan. In another bowl, beat egg yolks; add the sour cream and mix well. Set aside 6-8 peach slices for garnish. Cut remaining peaches into 1-in. pieces; stir into the sour cream mixture. Spread over crust; sprinkle with cinnamon.

Bake at 350° for 25-30 minutes or until the edges begin to brown. Cool completely on a wire rack. Spread with whipped topping; garnish with reserved peaches. Store in the refrigerator. **Yield:** 12 servings.

Banana Fudge Cake

Jan Gregory, Bethel, Ohio

(Pictured above and on page 4)

You'll love the banana flavor throughout this moist, fudgy cake and fluffy frosting. This recipe was given to me by my mother-in-law. It's a favorite at family gatherings.

1 package (18-1/4 ounces) chocolate fudge cake mix
1 large ripe banana, mashed
FROSTING:
1/2 cup butter *or* margarine
1/4 cup water
5-1/2 cups confectioners' sugar, *divided*
1/4 cup baking cocoa
1 small ripe banana, mashed
1/2 teaspoon vanilla extract

In a mixing bowl, prepare cake mix according to package directions, omitting 1/4 cup of the water. Beat on low speed until moistened. Add banana; beat on high for 2 minutes. Pour into a greased 13-in. x 9-in. x 2-in. baking pan. Bake at 350° for 35-40 minutes or until a toothpick inserted near the center comes out clean. Cool completely.

In a saucepan, heat butter and water until butter is melted; set aside. In a mixing bowl, combine 4 cups confectioners' sugar and cocoa. Add butter mixture, banana and vanilla; beat until smooth. Add enough remaining sugar until frosting reaches desired spreading consistency. Frost cake. **Yield:** 12-15 servings.

Did You Know?

ALTHOUGH the first cake mixes were not on grocery store shelves until after World War II, the mix has been evolving since the 1920s.

p. 35

p. 35

p. 36

p. 31

p. 29

Clockwise from top left: Apricot Torte, Easy Red Velvet Cake, Chocolate Raspberry Torte, Pumpkin-Pecan Cake and Cookies-and-Cream Cake.

Two-Layer Cakes & Tortes

Buttermilk Banana Cake

Arlene Grenz, Linton, North Dakota

(Pictured below)

When I was a girl, this was my family's favorite Sunday cake. Since I'm "nuts" about nuts, I added the pecans.

- 3/4 cup butter *or* margarine, softened
- 1 cup sugar
- 1/2 cup packed brown sugar
- 2 eggs
- 1 cup mashed ripe banana
- 1 teaspoon vanilla extract
- 2 cups cake flour
- 1 teaspoon baking powder
- 1 teaspoon baking soda
- 1/2 teaspoon salt
- 1/2 cup buttermilk

FILLING:
- 1/2 cup half-and-half cream
- 1/2 cup sugar
- 2 tablespoons butter *or* margarine
- 2 tablespoons all-purpose flour
- 1/4 teaspoon salt
- 1 teaspoon vanilla extract
- 1/2 cup chopped pecans

FROSTING:
- 2 cups whipping cream
- 1/4 cup confectioners' sugar

In a mixing bowl, cream butter and sugars until fluffy. Add eggs; beat for 2 minutes. Add banana and vanilla; beat for 2 minutes. Combine the flour, baking powder, baking soda and salt; add to creamed mixture alternately with buttermilk. Pour into two greased and floured 9-in. round baking pans. Bake at 375° for 25-30 minutes or until a toothpick inserted near the center comes out clean. Cool for 10 minutes before removing from pans to wire racks to cool completely.

For filling, combine half-and-half, sugar, butter, flour and salt in a saucepan. Bring to a boil; cook and stir for 2 minutes. Remove from the heat; stir in vanilla and pecans. Cool. Spread between cake layers.

For frosting, beat whipping cream until soft peaks form. Gradually beat in the confectioners' sugar; beat until stiff peaks form. Spread over top and sides of cake. Store in the refrigerator. **Yield:** 12-16 servings.

Sour Cream Chocolate Cake

Patsy Foster, Marion, Arkansas

(Pictured above)

This luscious chocolate layer cake gets wonderful moistness from sour cream. Its irresistible topping and marvelous from-scratch goodness make it a classic! I keep the recipe handy for birthdays and holidays.

- 4 squares (1 ounce *each*) unsweetened chocolate, melted and cooled
- 1 cup water
- 3/4 cup sour cream
- 1/4 cup shortening
- 1 teaspoon vanilla extract
- 2 eggs, beaten
- 2 cups all-purpose flour
- 2 cups sugar
- 1-1/4 teaspoons baking soda
- 1 teaspoon salt
- 1/2 teaspoon baking powder

FROSTING:
- 1/2 cup butter (no substitutes), softened
- 6 squares (1 ounce *each*) unsweetened chocolate, melted and cooled
- 6 cups confectioners' sugar
- 1/2 cup sour cream
- 6 tablespoons milk
- 2 teaspoons vanilla extract
- 1/8 teaspoon salt

In a mixing bowl, combine the first six ingredients; mix well. Combine the dry ingredients; gradually add to chocolate mixture. Beat on low speed just until moistened. Beat on high for 3 minutes. Pour into two greased and floured 9-in. round baking pans. Bake at 350° for 30 minutes or until a toothpick inserted near the center comes out clean. Cool for 10 minutes before removing from pans to wire racks to cool completely.

In a mixing bowl, combine frosting ingredients. Beat until smooth and creamy. Spread between layers and over top and sides of cake. Store in the refrigerator. **Yield:** 12-16 servings.

Toffee-Mocha Cream Torte

Lynn Rogers, Richfield, North Carolina

(Pictured below)

When you really want to impress someone, this scrumptious torte is just the thing to make! Instant coffee granules give the moist chocolate cake a mild mocha flavor...while the fluffy whipped cream layers, blended with brown sugar and crunchy toffee bits, are deliciously rich.

 1 cup butter *or* margarine, softened
 2 cups sugar
 2 eggs
 1-1/2 teaspoons vanilla extract
 2-2/3 cups all-purpose flour
 3/4 cup baking cocoa
 2 teaspoons baking soda
 1/4 teaspoon salt
 1 cup buttermilk
 2 teaspoons instant coffee granules
 1 cup boiling water
 TOPPING:
 1/2 teaspoon instant coffee granules
 1 teaspoon hot water
 2 cups whipping cream
 3 tablespoons light brown sugar
 6 Heath candy bars (1.4 ounces *each*),
 crushed, *divided*

In a mixing bowl, cream butter and sugar. Beat in eggs and vanilla. Combine the flour, cocoa, baking soda and salt; add to creamed mixture alternately with buttermilk. Dissolve coffee in water; add to batter. Beat for 2 minutes. Pour into three greased and floured 9-in. round baking pans. Bake at 350° for 16-20 minutes or until a toothpick inserted near the center comes out clean. Cool for 10 minutes before removing from pans to wire racks to cool completely.

For topping, dissolve coffee in water in a mixing bowl; cool. Add cream and brown sugar. Beat until stiff peaks form. Place bottom cake layer on a serving plate; top with 1-1/3 cups of topping. Sprinkle with 1/2 cup of crushed candy bars. Repeat layers twice. Store in the refrigerator. **Yield:** 12-14 servings.

Pretty Pineapple Torte

Iola Egle, McCook, Nebraska

(Pictured above)

Pineapple stars in both the cake and filling in this tall, beautiful dessert. It's creamy and just lightly sweet.

- 1/2 cup butter *or* margarine, softened
- 1 cup sugar, *divided*
- 3 eggs, *separated*
- 1 can (20 ounces) crushed pineapple
- 1 teaspoon vanilla extract
- 2-1/2 cups cake flour
- 2 teaspoons baking powder
- 1/2 teaspoon baking soda
- 1/2 teaspoon salt

FILLING:
- 1-1/2 cups whipping cream
- 1/4 cup confectioners' sugar
- 1/2 teaspoon almond extract
- 2 tablespoons slivered almonds, toasted

In a large mixing bowl, cream butter and 3/4 cup sugar. Beat in egg yolks. Drain pineapple, reserving 2/3 cup juice (discard remaining juice or save for another use). In a bowl, combine juice, 3/4 cup pineapple and vanilla (set remaining pineapple aside for filling). Combine dry ingredients; add to creamed mixture alternately with pineapple mixture. In a small mixing bowl, beat egg whites until soft peaks form. Add remaining sugar, 1 tablespoon at a time, beating until stiff peaks form. Fold a fourth of the egg whites into batter; fold in remaining whites. Spoon into two greased and floured 9-in. round baking pans. Bake at 350° for 28-32 minutes or until cake springs back when lightly touched. Cool for 10 minutes; remove from pans to wire racks to cool completely.

For filling, beat the cream, sugar and extract in a mixing bowl until stiff peaks form. Fold in reserved pineapple. Split each cake layer in half horizontally. Spread about 3/4 cup filling between each layer; spread remaining filling over the top. Sprinkle with almonds. Store in the refrigerator. **Yield:** 10-12 servings.

Mother's Walnut Cake

Helen Vail, Glenside, Pennsylvania

Even though Mother baked this tall, beautiful cake often when I was growing up, it was a real treat every time.

- 1/2 cup butter *or* margarine, softened
- 1/2 cup shortening
- 2 cups sugar
- 4 eggs
- 3-1/2 cups all-purpose flour
- 2 teaspoons baking soda
- 1/2 teaspoon salt
- 1-1/2 cups buttermilk
- 2 teaspoons vanilla extract
- 1-1/2 cups ground walnuts

FROSTING:
- 2 packages (one 8 ounces, one 3 ounces) cream cheese, softened
- 3/4 cup butter *or* margarine, softened
- 5 to 5-1/2 cups confectioners' sugar
- 1-1/2 teaspoons vanilla extract
- 1/3 cup finely chopped walnuts

In a large mixing bowl, cream butter, shortening and sugar. Add eggs, one at a time, beating well after each addition. Combine flour, baking soda and salt; add to the creamed mixture alternately with buttermilk and vanilla. Beat on low speed just until combined. Stir in the walnuts. Pour into three greased and floured 9-in. round baking pans. Bake at 350° for 20-25 minutes or until a toothpick inserted near the center comes out clean. Cool for 5 minutes before removing from pans to wire racks to cool completely.

For frosting, beat cream cheese and butter in a mixing bowl. Add sugar; mix well. Add vanilla; beat until smooth. Spread between layers and over top and sides of cake. Sprinkle with walnuts. Store in the refrigerator. **Yield:** 12-16 servings.

Lime Cream Torte

Theresa Tometich, Coralville, Iowa

This impressive-looking dessert is surprisingly simple to prepare. Light and refreshing, it's a super make-ahead treat—the flavor gets better as it sits in the refrigerator.

- 1 package (18-1/4 ounces) butter recipe golden cake mix*
- 3 eggs
- 1/2 cup butter *or* margarine, softened
- 7 tablespoons water
- 3 tablespoons lime juice

FILLING:
- 1 can (14 ounces) sweetened condensed milk
- 1/2 cup lime juice
- 2 cups whipping cream, whipped

In a mixing bowl, combine dry cake mix, eggs, butter, water and lime juice. Beat on medium speed for 4 minutes. Pour into two greased and floured 9-in. round baking pans. Bake at 375° for 20-25 minutes or until a toothpick inserted near the center comes out clean. Cool for 10 minutes before removing from pans to wire racks.

When cool, split each cake into two horizontal layers. In a bowl, combine milk and lime juice. Fold in the whipped cream. Spread about 1-1/4 cups between each layer and over top of cake. Chill for at least 1 hour. Store in the refrigerator. **Yield:** 10-14 servings.

*Editor's Note: This recipe was tested with Duncan Hines Butter Recipe Golden Cake mix.

Banana Nut Layer Cake

Patsy Howard, Bakersfield, California

(Pictured below)

This cake is the top choice of the "birthday child" in our family! It's been a favorite for years.

      1/2 cup shortening
      2 cups sugar
      1 egg plus 1 egg white
      1 cup buttermilk
      1 cup mashed ripe bananas
      2 cups all-purpose flour
      1 teaspoon baking soda
      1 teaspoon salt
      1 teaspoon vanilla extract
   1/2 cup chopped walnuts
FILLING:
   1/4 cup butter *or* margarine
   1/2 cup packed brown sugar
   1/4 cup all-purpose flour
Pinch salt
      3/4 cup milk
      1 egg yolk
      1 teaspoon vanilla extract
   1/2 cup chopped walnuts
Confectioners' sugar

In a mixing bowl, cream shortening and sugar. Beat in egg and egg white. Add buttermilk and bananas; mix well. Combine flour, baking soda and salt; stir into the creamed mixture. Add vanilla and nuts. Pour into two greased and floured 9-in. round baking pans. Bake at 350° for 35 minutes or until a toothpick inserted near the center comes out clean. Cool for 10 minutes before removing from pans to wire racks to cool completely.

For filling, melt butter and brown sugar in a saucepan over medium heat. In a small bowl, combine flour and salt with a small amount of milk; stir until smooth. Add remaining milk gradually. Add egg yolk and mix well; stir into saucepan. Cook and stir over medium heat until very thick, about 10 minutes. Add vanilla and nuts. Cool. Spread between cake layers. Dust with confectioners' sugar. Store in the refrigerator. **Yield:** 10-12 servings.

Cookies-and-Cream Cake

Pat Habiger, Spearville, Kansas

(Pictured above and on page 24)

The taste of this moist, fun-to-eat cake will remind you of Oreo cookies.

      1 package (18-1/4 ounces) white cake mix
1-1/4 cups water
   1/3 cup vegetable oil
      3 egg whites
      1 cup coarsely crushed cream-filled chocolate
         sandwich cookies (about 8)
FROSTING:
      4 to 4-1/2 cups confectioners' sugar
   1/2 cup shortening
   1/4 cup milk
      1 teaspoon vanilla extract
Additional cream-filled chocolate sandwich
   cookies, halved *and/or* crushed, optional

In a large mixing bowl, combine cake mix, water, oil and egg whites. Beat on low speed until moistened; beat on high for 2 minutes. Gently fold in crushed cookies. Pour into two greased and floured 8-in. round baking pans. Bake at 350° for 30 minutes or until a toothpick inserted in center comes out clean. Cool for 10 minutes; remove from pans to wire racks to cool completely.

In a mixing bowl, beat sugar, shortening, milk and vanilla until smooth. Frost cake. If desired, decorate the top with cookie halves and the sides with crushed cookies. **Yield:** 12 servings.

29

Raspberry Walnut Torte

Bonnie Malloy, Norwood, Pennsylvania

(Pictured below)

I often serve this impressive cake for dinner parties or whenever a special dessert is called for. It's delicious and also very pretty. It takes a little time to prepare but is well worth the extra effort.

- 1-1/2 cups whipping cream
- 3 eggs
- 1-1/2 cups sugar
- 3 teaspoons vanilla extract
- 1-3/4 cups all-purpose flour
- 1 cup ground walnuts, toasted
- 2 teaspoons baking powder
- 1/2 teaspoon salt

FROSTING:

- 1-1/2 cups whipping cream
- 1 package (8 ounces) cream cheese, softened
- 1 cup sugar
- 1/8 teaspoon salt
- 1 teaspoon vanilla extract
- 1 jar (12 ounces) raspberry preserves

In a small mixing bowl, beat cream until stiff peaks form; set aside. In a large mixing bowl, beat eggs, sugar and vanilla until thick and lemon-colored. Combine flour, walnuts, baking powder and salt; fold into egg mixture alternately with whipped cream. Pour into two greased and floured 9-in. round baking pans. Bake at 350° for 25- 30 minutes or until a toothpick inserted near the center comes out clean. Cool for 10 minutes before removing from pans to wire racks to cool completely.

In a small mixing bowl, beat cream until stiff peaks form; set aside. In a large mixing bowl, beat cream cheese, sugar and salt until fluffy. Add vanilla; mix well. Fold in whipped cream.

Split each cake into two layers. Place bottom layer on serving plate; spread with about 1/2 cup frosting. Top with second cake layer; spread with half of the raspberry preserves. Repeat layers. Frost sides of cake with frosting.

Cut a small hole in the corner of a pastry or plastic bag; insert ribbon tip #47. Fill bag with remaining frosting; pipe a lattice design on top of cake. Using star tip #32, pipe stars around top and bottom edges of cake. Store in the refrigerator. **Yield:** 16 servings.

Editor's Note: A coupler ring will allow you to easily change tips for different designs.

Pastry Bag Pointer

PACK FROSTING to the bottom of the pastry bag to prevent air bubbles. Squeeze out a little frosting before starting to decorate.

Pumpkin-Pecan Cake

Joyce Platfoot, Wapakoneta, Ohio

(Pictured above and on page 24)

With our eight children, I do a lot of cooking. But I have to admit, I enjoy baking much more. This cake is one of my family's favorites.

        2 cups crushed vanilla wafers (about 50)
        1 cup chopped pecans
      3/4 cup butter *or* margarine, softened
    CAKE:
        1 package (18-1/4 ounces) spice cake mix
        1 can (15 ounces) solid-pack pumpkin
      1/4 cup butter *or* margarine, softened
        4 eggs
    FILLING/TOPPING:
      2/3 cup butter *or* margarine, softened
        1 package (3 ounces) cream cheese, softened
        3 cups confectioners' sugar
        2 teaspoons vanilla extract
      1/2 cup caramel ice cream topping

In a mixing bowl on medium speed, beat the wafers, pecans and butter until crumbly, about 1 minute. Press into three greased and floured 9-in. round baking pans. In another mixing bowl, beat cake mix, pumpkin, butter and eggs for 3 minutes. Spread over crust in each pan. Bake at 350° for 30 minutes or until a toothpick inserted near the center comes out clean. Cool for 10 minutes before removing from pans to wire racks to cool completely.

For filling, combine butter and cream cheese in a small mixing bowl. Add sugar and vanilla; beat on medium until light and fluffy, about 3 minutes. Thinly spread between layers (crumb side down) and on the sides of cake. Spread caramel topping over top of cake, allowing some to drip down the sides. Store in the refrigerator. **Yield:** 16-20 servings.

Strawberry Meringue Cake

Dorothy Anderson, Ottawa, Kansas

(Pictured below)

Guests say "Wow!" when I present this torte. Mashed berries add flavor to the cream filling.

        1 package (18-1/4 ounces) yellow cake mix
    1-1/3 cups orange juice
        4 eggs, *separated*
    1-1/2 teaspoons grated orange peel
      1/4 teaspoon cream of tartar
        1 cup plus 1/4 cup sugar, *divided*
        2 cups whipping cream
        2 pints fresh strawberries, *divided*

In a mixing bowl, combine cake mix, orange juice, egg yolks and orange peel. Beat on medium speed for 4 minutes. Pour into two greased and floured 9-in. round baking pans; set aside. In a mixing bowl, beat egg whites and cream of tartar on medium until foamy. Gradually beat in 1 cup sugar, a tablespoon at a time, on high until stiff glossy peaks form and sugar is dissolved. Spread the meringue evenly over cake batter. Bake at 350° for 35 minutes or until meringue is lightly browned. Cool in pans on wire racks (meringue will crack).

Beat cream until stiff peaks form. Mash 1/2 cup of strawberries with remaining sugar; fold into whipped cream. Loosen edges of cakes from pans with a knife. Using two large spatulas, carefully remove one cake to a serving platter, meringue side up. Carefully spread with about two-thirds of the cream mixture. Slice the remaining strawberries; arrange half over cream mixture. Repeat layers. Store in the refrigerator. **Yield:** 12-16 servings.

cake into two layers. Spread filling between layers and over sides of torte. Spread jam over top. Garnish with whipped cream, apricots and hazelnuts if desired. Store in the refrigerator. **Yield:** 12-14 servings.

Raisin-Filled Torte

Jo Peapples, Brooksville, Florida

(Pictured below)

My mother used this recipe many times when I was growing up, and it was always my favorite. She's gone now, but her memory lingers each time I bake this cake. The layers are different flavors, and combined they're deliciously unique. Every time I serve it, I have to send my guests home with the recipe!

        1/2 cup shortening
    1-1/4 cups sugar
        2 eggs
        2 cups cake flour
        2 teaspoons baking powder
        3/4 teaspoon salt
        3/4 cup milk
        1 teaspoon vanilla extract
    1-1/2 teaspoons maple syrup
        1/4 teaspoon ground cinnamon
        1/8 teaspoon ground cloves
        1/8 teaspoon ground nutmeg
    FILLING:
        1/3 cup sugar
        1 tablespoon cornstarch
        2/3 cup water
    1-1/2 cups raisins
        1 teaspoon lemon juice
        1 teaspoon butter *or* margarine
        1/4 teaspoon grated lemon peel
    ICING:
        1 cup confectioners' sugar
        1 tablespoon butter *or* margarine, melted
        1/4 teaspoon grated lemon peel
        5 to 6 teaspoons milk

Apricot Hazelnut Torte

Enid Stoehr, Emsdale, Ontario

(Pictured above)

My husband, Gerry, and I love it when our children and grandchildren visit. One cake that gets "oohs" and "aahs" from the family every time is this luscious torte. It's as light as a feather and tastes heavenly. Plus, it looks so beautiful, it's perfect for special occasions.

        1 cup ground hazelnuts
        3/4 cup all-purpose flour
        2 teaspoons baking powder
        1/2 teaspoon salt
        4 eggs, *separated*
        2 tablespoons water
        1 teaspoon vanilla extract
        1 cup sugar, *divided*
        2 cups whipping cream
        1/4 cup confectioners' sugar
        2/3 cup pureed canned apricots
        1/2 cup apricot jam, warmed
    Whipped cream, sliced apricots and whole *or*
        chopped hazelnuts, optional

In a bowl, combine hazelnuts, flour, baking powder and salt; set aside. In a mixing bowl, beat the egg yolks, water and vanilla until lemon-colored. Gradually add 3/4 cup sugar; set aside.

In another mixing bowl, beat egg whites until soft peaks form. Add remaining sugar, 1 tablespoon at a time, beating until stiff peaks form. Fold a fourth of the dry ingredients into egg yolk mixture. Repeat three times. Fold in egg white mixture. Line two greased 9-in. round baking pans with waxed paper; grease the paper. Spread batter evenly into pans. Bake at 350° for 20-25 minutes or until cake springs back when lightly touched. Cool for 10 minutes before removing from pans to wire racks to cool completely.

In a mixing bowl, beat cream and confectioners' sugar until stiff peaks form. Fold in apricots. Split each

In a mixing bowl, cream shortening and sugar. Add eggs, one at a time, beating well after each. Combine flour, baking powder and salt; add to creamed mixture alternately with milk. Pour half of the batter into another bowl. Add vanilla to one bowl; add syrup, cinnamon, cloves and nutmeg to the second bowl. Pour each batter into a greased and floured 9-in. round baking pan. Bake at 375° for 20-25 minutes or until a toothpick inserted near the center comes out clean. Cool for 10 minutes before removing from pans to wire racks to cool completely.

Combine sugar and cornstarch in a saucepan; stir in water until smooth. Add raisins. Bring to a boil; boil and stir for 2 minutes. Remove from the heat; stir in lemon juice, butter and peel. Cool. In a small bowl, whisk sugar, butter and lemon peel. Add milk until icing reaches desired consistency. Place the spice cake layer on a serving platter; spread with filling. Top with vanilla cake layer and icing. **Yield:** 12 servings.

Moist Chocolate Cake
(Pictured on front cover)

This dark, moist cake developed by our Test Kitchen is perfect for birthdays. The basic buttery frosting has an unmatchable homemade taste. With a few simple variations, you can come up with different colors and flavors.

    2 cups all-purpose flour
    2 cups sugar
 3/4 cup unsweetened cocoa
    2 teaspoons baking soda
    1 teaspoon salt
    1 teaspoon baking powder
    1 cup vegetable oil
    1 cup brewed coffee, room temperature
    1 cup milk
    2 eggs
    1 teaspoon vanilla extract
BUTTERCREAM FROSTING:
    1 cup butter (no substitutes), softened
    8 cups confectioners' sugar
    2 teaspoons vanilla extract
    1/2 to 3/4 cup milk

In a mixing bowl, combine the first six ingredients. Add oil, coffee and milk; beat at medium speed for 2 minutes. Add eggs and vanilla; beat 2 minutes more. Pour into two greased and floured 9-in. round baking pans. Bake at 325° for 25-30 minutes or until a toothpick inserted near the center comes out clean. Cool in pans for 10 minutes before removing to wire racks to cool completely.

For frosting, in a mixing bowl, cream butter. Beat in sugar and vanilla. Add milk until frosting reaches desired consistency. Spread frosting between layers and over top and sides of cake. **Yield:** 12 servings.

For chocolate frosting: Substitute 1/2 cup baking cocoa for 1/2 cup of the confectioners' sugar.

For peanut butter frosting: Substitute peanut butter for the butter.

Praline Pumpkin Torte
Esther Sinn, Princeton, Illinois
(Pictured above)

This favorite harvest cake stays moist to the last bite. It's perfect for Thanksgiving or Christmas gatherings.

 3/4 cup packed brown sugar
 1/3 cup butter (no substitutes)
    3 tablespoons whipping cream
 3/4 cup chopped pecans
CAKE:
    4 eggs
 1-2/3 cups sugar
    1 cup vegetable oil
    2 cups cooked *or* canned pumpkin
 1/4 teaspoon vanilla extract
    2 cups all-purpose flour
    2 teaspoons baking powder
    2 teaspoons pumpkin pie spice
    1 teaspoon baking soda
    1 teaspoon salt
TOPPING:
 1-3/4 cups whipping cream
 1/4 cup confectioners' sugar
 1/4 teaspoon vanilla extract
Additional chopped pecans

In a heavy saucepan, combine brown sugar, butter and cream. Cook and stir over low heat until sugar is dissolved. Pour into two well-greased 9-in. round baking pans. Sprinkle with pecans; cool. In a mixing bowl, beat eggs, sugar, oil, pumpkin and vanilla. Combine dry ingredients; add to pumpkin mixture; beat just until blended. Carefully spoon over brown sugar mixture. Bake at 350° for 30-35 minutes or until a toothpick inserted near the center comes out clean. Cool for 5 minutes before removing from pans to wire racks to cool completely.

Place one cake layer on a serving plate. In a mixing bowl, beat cream until soft peaks form. Beat in sugar and vanilla. Spread two-thirds over cake. Top with second cake layer, whipped cream and pecans. Store in the refrigerator. **Yield:** 12-14 servings.

Butter Pecan Cake

Becky Miller, Tallahassee, Florida

(Pictured below)

This cake is one that my family's enjoyed for many years, especially at Thanksgiving and Christmas.

2-2/3 cups chopped pecans
1-1/4 cups butter (no substitutes), softened, *divided*
    2 cups sugar
    4 eggs
    3 cups all-purpose flour
    2 teaspoons baking powder
1/2 teaspoon salt
    1 cup milk
    2 teaspoons vanilla extract
FROSTING:
    1 cup butter, softened
    8 to 8-1/2 cups confectioners' sugar
    1 can (5 ounces) evaporated milk
    2 teaspoons vanilla extract

Place pecans and 1/4 cup of butter in a baking pan. Bake at 350° for 20-25 minutes or until toasted, stirring frequently; set aside. In a mixing bowl, cream sugar and remaining butter. Add eggs, one at a time, beating well after each addition. Combine flour, baking powder and salt; add to the creamed mixture alternately with milk. Stir in vanilla and 1-1/3 cups of toasted pecans. Pour into three greased and floured 9-in. round baking pans. Bake at 350° for 25-30 minutes. Cool for 10 minutes before removing from pans to wire racks to cool completely.

For frosting, cream butter and sugar in a mixing bowl. Add milk and vanilla; beat until smooth. Stir in remaining toasted pecans. Spread frosting between layers and over top and sides of cake. **Yield:** 12-16 servings.

Butternut Squash Layer Cake

Deanna Richter, Fenton, Iowa

The recipe for this lovely tall cake with its yummy old-fashioned frosting has been in our family for as long as I can remember. I like to make it throughout the year but typically in the cooler fall months.

1/2 cup butter *or* margarine, softened
    1 cup sugar
    1 cup packed brown sugar
    2 eggs
    1 cup mashed cooked butternut squash
    1 teaspoon maple flavoring
    3 cups cake flour
    4 teaspoons baking powder
1/4 teaspoon baking soda
1/2 cup milk
    1 cup chopped walnuts
BROWN SUGAR FROSTING:
1-1/2 cups packed brown sugar
    3 egg whites
    6 tablespoons water
1/4 teaspoon cream of tartar
1/8 teaspoon salt
    1 teaspoon vanilla extract

In a mixing bowl, cream the butter and sugars. Add eggs, one at a time, beating well after each addition. Add squash and maple flavoring; mix well. Combine flour, baking powder and baking soda; add to creamed mixture alternately with milk. Stir in walnuts. Pour into two greased and floured 9-in. round baking pans. Bake at 350° for 25-30 minutes or until a toothpick inserted near the center comes out clean. Cool 10 minutes before removing from pans to wire racks to cool completely.

For frosting, combine the brown sugar, egg whites, water, cream of tartar and salt in a heavy saucepan. With a portable mixer, beat on low speed for 1 minute. Continue beating over low heat until a thermometer reads 160°, about 8-10 minutes.

Pour frosting into a large mixing bowl; add vanilla. Beat on high speed until stiff peaks form, about 3 minutes. Spread between layers and over top and sides of cake. Store in the refrigerator. **Yield:** 10-12 servings.

Editor's Note: A stand mixer is recommended for beating the frosting after it reaches 160°.

Best Baking Pans

DULL ALUMINUM baking pans are best for making cakes. They reflect heat away from the cake and give it a tender, light-brown crust.

Easy Red Velvet Cake

Priscilla Weaver, Hagerstown, Maryland

(Pictured above and on page 24)

I've been making this cake for many years, trying slight changes in the recipe until coming up with one I consider "tried and proven".

    1 package (18-1/4 ounces) fudge marble
      cake mix
    1 teaspoon baking soda
    2 eggs
1-1/2 cups buttermilk
    1 bottle (1 ounce) red food coloring
    1 teaspoon vanilla extract
FROSTING:
    5 tablespoons all-purpose flour
    1 cup milk
    1 cup butter *or* margarine, softened
    1 cup sugar
    2 teaspoons vanilla extract

In a mixing bowl, combine contents of cake mix and baking soda. Add eggs, buttermilk, food coloring and vanilla; blend on low until moistened. Beat on high speed for 2 minutes. Pour into two greased and floured 9-in. round baking pans. Bake at 350° for 30-35 minutes or until a toothpick inserted near the center comes out clean. Cool for 10 minutes before removing from pans to wire racks to cool completely.

For frosting, whisk flour and milk in a saucepan until smooth. Bring to a boil; cook and stir for 2 minutes or until thickened. Cover and cool to room temperature. In a mixing bowl, cream butter and sugar. Add milk mixture; beat for 10 minutes or until fluffy. Stir in vanilla. Frost between layers and over top and sides of cake. **Yield:** 12 servings.

Apricot Torte

Dorothy Pritchett, Wills Point, Texas

(Pictured below and on page 24)

This yummy dessert is simple to assemble and oh-so-pretty. I serve it often to guests.

    6 eggs, *separated*
1/2 cup plus 5 tablespoons sugar, *divided*
    1 cup all-purpose flour
CHOCOLATE BUTTERCREAM:
    1/4 cup sugar
    3 eggs plus 2 egg yolks
    1 teaspoon vanilla extract
    1 teaspoon instant coffee granules
    2 squares (1 ounce *each*) semisweet
      chocolate
    1 cup butter (no substitutes), softened
APRICOT FILLING:
    2 cans (17 ounces *each*) apricot halves,
      drained
    1 cup apricot preserves
Chocolate curls, optional

In a large mixing bowl, beat egg yolks and 1/2 cup sugar until thickened. In a small mixing bowl, beat egg whites until foamy. Gradually add remaining sugar, beating until stiff peaks form. Fold into yolk mixture. Gradually fold in flour. Divide batter between three greased and floured 9-in. round baking pans. Bake at 350° for 15 minutes or until golden. Cool for 5 minutes before removing from pans to wire racks to cool completely.

For buttercream, whisk sugar, eggs, yolks, vanilla and coffee in a saucepan. Add chocolate; cook and stir over low heat until thickened (do not boil). Cool completely.

In a mixing bowl, cream butter. Gradually add chocolate mixture; set aside. Finely chop apricots; drain and place in a bowl. Stir in preserves; set aside.

Split each cake into two horizontal layers; place one on a serving plate. Spread with 2/3 cup buttercream. Top with another cake layer and 2/3 cup apricot filling. Repeat layers twice. Cover and refrigerate 3 hours before serving. Garnish with chocolate curls if desired. **Yield:** 12 servings.

Chocolate Raspberry Torte

Rosemary Ford Vinson, El Cajon, California

(Pictured above and on page 24)

When our daughter requested this fancy layered cake for her birthday, I was afraid it would be difficult to make. But it's so easy!

- 1 package (18-1/4 ounces) chocolate cake mix
- 1 package (3 ounces) cream cheese, softened
- 3/4 cup cold milk
- 1 package (3.4 ounces) instant vanilla pudding mix
- 1 carton (8 ounces) frozen whipped topping, thawed
- 2 cups fresh raspberries

Confectioners' sugar
Fresh mint and additional raspberries, optional

Prepare cake according to package directions, using three greased and floured 9-in. round baking pans. Bake at 350° for 25-30 minutes or until a toothpick inserted near center comes out clean. Cool for 10 minutes; remove from pans to wire racks to cool completely.

In a mixing bowl, beat cream cheese until fluffy. Combine milk and pudding mix; add to cream cheese and mix well. Fold in whipped topping and raspberries. Place one cake layer on a serving plate. Spread with half of the filling. Repeat layers. Top with remaining cake; dust with confectioners' sugar. Garnish with mint and raspberries if desired. Store in the refrigerator. **Yield:** 12 servings.

Butterscotch Torte

Lavonne Hartel, Williston, North Dakota

(Pictured at right)

It's best to make the graham cracker cake for this torte the day before, because the flavor improves as it mellows. The recipe makes plenty of yummy butterscotch sauce, so you can drizzle some over the top and have extra to serve on the side.

- 6 eggs, *separated*
- 1-1/2 cups sugar
- 2 teaspoons vanilla extract
- 2 cups graham cracker crumbs
- 1 cup finely chopped nuts
- 1 teaspoon baking powder

TOPPING/FILLING:
- 1 cup packed brown sugar
- 1 tablespoon all-purpose flour

Dash salt
- 1/4 cup orange juice
- 2 tablespoons water
- 1 egg, beaten
- 1/4 cup butter *or* margarine
- 1 teaspoon vanilla extract
- 2 cups whipping cream
- 1/4 cup confectioners' sugar

Line three greased 9-in. round baking pans with waxed paper and grease the paper; set aside. In a small mixing bowl, beat egg whites on high speed until stiff peaks form; set aside. In a large mixing bowl, beat egg yolks and sugar until thick and lemon-colored. Add vanilla; mix well. Combine the cracker crumbs, nuts and baking powder; fold into egg yolk mixture. Gradually fold in egg whites. Pour into prepared pans. Bake at 325° for 20-25 minutes or until lightly browned. Cool for 10 minutes before removing from pans to wire racks to cool completely.

For topping, combine brown sugar, flour and salt in a saucepan. Stir in orange juice and water until smooth; bring to a boil. Reduce heat; cook and stir for 2 minutes or until slightly thickened. Stir some of the hot mixture into beaten egg; return to the pan, stirring constantly. Cook and stir until nearly boiling; reduce heat. Cook and stir 1-2 minutes longer (do not boil). Remove from heat; stir in butter and vanilla. Cool completely.

In a mixing bowl, beat cream until soft peaks form. Beat in confectioners' sugar until stiff. Place one cake layer on a serving plate; spread with a third of the whipped cream. Repeat layers twice. Drizzle some of the topping over cake. Serve remaining topping with cake. Store in the refrigerator. **Yield:** 12 servings.

Orange Dream Cake
Willa Govoro, St. Clair, Missouri
(Pictured above)

The flavor of orange and lemon really comes through in this pretty cake. With a heavenly whipped cream frosting, it's a delightful end to any meal.

> 2/3 cup butter *or* margarine, softened
> 1-1/3 cups sugar
> 2/3 cup fresh orange juice
> 3 tablespoons fresh lemon juice
> 1 teaspoon grated orange peel
> 1 teaspoon grated lemon peel
> 2 eggs
> 2 cups cake flour
> 2 teaspoons baking powder
> 1 teaspoon salt

FROSTING:
> 1 cup flaked coconut
> 1/4 cup sugar
> 2 tablespoons fresh orange juice
> 1 tablespoon fresh lemon juice
> 4 teaspoons grated orange peel, *divided*
> 1 cup whipping cream, whipped

In a large mixing bowl, cream butter and sugar. Add juices and peel; mix well (mixture may appear curdled). Add eggs, one at a time, beating well after each addition. Sift flour with baking powder and salt; add to creamed mixture and mix well. Pour into two greased and floured 8-in. round baking pans. Bake at 375° for 25-30 minutes or until a toothpick inserted near the center comes out clean. Cool in pans for 10 minutes before removing to wire racks to cool completely.

For frosting, combine coconut, sugar, juices and 3 teaspoons peel; mix well. Let stand for 10-15 minutes or until sugar is dissolved. Fold in whipped cream. Spread between cake layers and over the top. Sprinkle with remaining orange peel. Chill for at least 1 hour. Store in the refrigerator. **Yield:** 10-12 servings.

Peanut Butter Lover's Cake

Teresa Mozingo, Camden, South Carolina

(Pictured above)

My family thrives on peanut butter, so they just love it when I make this recipe.

   3 eggs
1-2/3 cups sugar, *divided*
1-1/2 cups milk, *divided*
   3 squares (1 ounce *each***) unsweetened chocolate, finely chopped**
  1/2 cup shortening
   1 teaspoon vanilla extract
   2 cups cake flour
   1 teaspoon baking soda
  1/2 teaspoon salt
PEANUT BUTTER FROSTING:
   2 packages (8 ounces *each***) cream cheese, softened**
   1 can (14 ounces) sweetened condensed milk
1-1/2 cups peanut butter
  1/4 cup salted peanuts, chopped
   3 milk chocolate candy bars (1.55 ounces *each***), broken into squares**

In a saucepan, whisk 1 egg until blended. Stir in 2/3 cup sugar, 1/2 cup milk and chocolate. Cook and stir over medium heat until chocolate melts and mixture comes to a boil. Remove from the heat; cool to room temperature.

In a mixing bowl, cream shortening and remaining sugar. Add remaining eggs, one at a time, beating well after each. Beat in vanilla. Combine the flour, baking soda and salt; add to creamed mixture alternately with remaining milk. Add chocolate mixture; mix well. Pour into three greased and floured 9-in. round baking pans. Bake at 325° for 25-30 minutes or until a toothpick inserted near the center comes out clean. Cool for 10 minutes before removing from pans to wire racks to cool completely.

For frosting, in a mixing bowl, beat cream cheese until light and fluffy. Gradually add milk and peanut butter, beating well after each addition. Spread between layers and over top and sides of cake. Sprinkle with peanuts. Garnish with candy bars. Store in the refrigerator. **Yield:** 12-14 servings.

Carrot Layer Cake

Linda Van Holland, Innisfail, Alberta

(Pictured below)

When they cut into it, people are bowled over by this moist, not-to-sweet cake. The pecan filling is another unexpected treat. My sister gave me the recipe.

FILLING:
   1 cup sugar
   2 tablespoons all-purpose flour
  1/4 teaspoon salt
   1 cup whipping cream
  1/2 cup butter *or* **margarine**
   1 cup chopped pecans
   1 teaspoon vanilla extract
CAKE:
1-1/4 cups vegetable oil
   2 cups sugar
   2 cups all-purpose flour
   2 teaspoons ground cinnamon
   2 teaspoons baking powder
   1 teaspoon baking soda
   1 teaspoon salt
   4 eggs
   4 cups finely shredded carrots
   1 cup raisins
   1 cup chopped pecans
FROSTING:
  3/4 cup butter *or* **margarine, softened**
   2 packages (3 ounces *each***) cream cheese, softened**
   1 teaspoon vanilla extract
   3 cups confectioners' sugar

In a heavy saucepan, combine sugar, flour and salt. Stir in cream; add butter. Cook and stir over medium heat until the butter is melted; bring to a boil. Reduce heat. Simmer, uncovered, for 30 minutes, stirring occasionally. Stir in nuts and vanilla. Set aside to cool.

In a mixing bowl, beat oil and sugar for 1 minute. Combine flour, cinnamon, baking powder, baking soda and salt; add to the creamed mixture alternately with eggs. Mix well. Stir in carrots, raisins and nuts. Pour into three greased and floured 9-in. round baking pans. Bake at 350° for 35-40 minutes or until a toothpick inserted near the center comes out clean. Cool in pans 10 minutes; remove to wire racks and cool completely.

For frosting, beat butter, cream cheese and vanilla until smooth. Gradually beat in sugar. Spread filling between cake layers. Frost sides and top of cake. Store in the refrigerator. **Yield:** 16-20 servings.

Sunny Coconut Cake

Annette Buckner, Charlotte, North Carolina

I've been making this easy cake for over 15 years and get many requests for the recipe.

- **2 cups (16 ounces) sour cream**
- **2 cups sugar**
- **1/4 cup orange juice**
- **1 package (14 ounces) flaked coconut**
- **1 package (18-1/4 ounces) yellow cake mix**
- **1 package (3 ounces) orange gelatin**
- **1 cup water**
- **1/3 cup vegetable oil**
- **2 eggs**
- **1 cup whipping cream**
- **1 can (11 ounces) mandarin oranges, well drained**

In a mixing bowl, combine sour cream, sugar and orange juice. Beat in coconut. Cover and refrigerate. In another mixing bowl, combine the cake mix, gelatin, water, oil and eggs; mix well. Pour into two greased and floured 9-in. round baking pans. Bake at 350° for 30-35 minutes or until a toothpick inserted near the center comes out clean. Cool for 10 minutes before removing from pans to wire racks to cool completely.

Split cakes in half. Set aside 1 cup of the coconut filling; spread remaining filling between cake layers. Refrigerate. Beat cream until stiff peaks form; fold into reserved filling. Frost top and sides of cake; garnish with oranges. Store in the refrigerator. **Yield:** 12-16 servings.

Eggnog Cake

Edith Disch, Fairview Park, Ohio

(Pictured above right)

With its moist cake layers, creamy filling and chocolate frosting, this cake appeals to all palates!

- **1/2 cup butter (no substitutes), softened**
- **1 cup sugar, *divided***
- **2 eggs, *separated***
- **3/4 cup orange juice**
- **1-1/2 teaspoons grated orange peel**
- **1 teaspoon vanilla extract**

- **2 cups sifted cake flour**
- **2 teaspoons baking powder**
- **1/2 teaspoon ground nutmeg**
- **1/4 teaspoon baking soda**
- **1/4 teaspoon salt**
- **EGGNOG FILLING:**
  - **5 tablespoons all-purpose flour**
  - **1-1/4 cups store-bought eggnog**
  - **1 cup butter, softened**
  - **3/4 cup sugar**
  - **1 teaspoon vanilla extract**
  - **1/4 teaspoon ground nutmeg**
- **CHOCOLATE FROSTING:**
  - **2 ounces unsweetened chocolate, melted**
  - **2/3 cup confectioners' sugar**
  - **1/4 teaspoon ground cinnamon**
  - **1/8 teaspoon ground nutmeg**
  - **3 tablespoons butter, softened**
  - **2 tablespoons whipping cream**
  - **2 to 3 tablespoons hot water**

Cream butter and 3/4 cup sugar. Add yolks, one at a time, beating well after each. Combine orange juice, peel and vanilla. Combine dry ingredients; add to creamed mixture alternately with juice mixture, beating well. In another bowl, beat whites until foamy; gradually add remaining sugar, beating until soft peaks form. Fold into batter. Line two greased 9-in. round baking pans with waxed paper; grease paper. Pour batter into pans. Bake at 350° for 20 minutes or until a toothpick inserted near the center comes out clean. Cool 5 minutes; remove to wire rack. Peel off paper; cool completely.

For filling, combine flour and a small amount of eggnog in a pan; stir until smooth. Stir in remaining eggnog; bring to a boil, stirring constantly. Cook and stir 2 minutes. Cool completely. Cream butter and sugar; add vanilla and nutmeg. Gradually beat in eggnog mixture.

For frosting, mix chocolate, sugar, cinnamon and nutmeg. Beat in butter and cream. Add water until frosting drizzles slightly. Split cakes in half; spread filling on three layers. Stack with plain layer on top; frost the top. Store in the refrigerator. **Yield:** 14 servings.

Maple Nut Cake

Emma Magielda, Amsterdam, New York

(Pictured below)

Our state is famous for its maple syrup. I like using maple syrup in desserts because it lends a distinct flavor.

   1/2 cup butter *or* margarine, softened
   1/2 cup sugar
     1 cup maple syrup
     2 eggs
2-1/4 cups cake flour
     3 teaspoons baking powder
     1 teaspoon salt
   1/2 cup milk
   1/2 cup chopped nuts
FROSTING:
     1 cup sugar
   1/2 cup maple syrup
     2 egg whites
     1 teaspoon corn syrup
   1/8 teaspoon salt
   1/4 teaspoon cream of tartar

In a bowl, cream the butter, sugar, syrup and eggs. Combine flour, baking powder and salt; add to the creamed mixture alternately with milk. Fold in nuts. Pour into two greased and floured 8-in. round baking pans. Bake at 350° for 20-25 minutes or until a toothpick inserted near the center comes out clean. Cool for 10 minutes before removing from pans to wire racks to cool completely.

In a heavy saucepan or double boiler, combine the frosting ingredients. With a portable mixer, beat on low speed for 1 minute. Continue beating over low heat until a thermometer reads 160°, about 8-10 minutes. Pour frosting into a large mixing bowl. Beat on high until stiff peaks form, about 3 minutes. Spread between layers and over top and sides of cake. **Yield:** 12-14 servings.

*Editor's Note: A stand mixer is recommended for beating the frosting after it reaches 160°.

Banana Pecan Torte

Linda Fryar, Stanton, Texas

(Pictured above)

The state tree of Texas is the pecan tree, so this recipe is popular around here. A friend shared the recipe with me. It's been in her family for years and years.

     1 cup butter *or* margarine, softened
2-1/2 cups sugar
     4 eggs
     2 cups mashed ripe bananas (about 4 medium)
     2 teaspoons vanilla extract
3-1/2 cups all-purpose flour
     2 teaspoons baking soda
   3/4 teaspoon salt
   1/2 cup buttermilk
     1 cup chopped pecans, toasted
FROSTING:
     1 package (8 ounces) cream cheese, softened
   1/2 cup butter *or* margarine, softened
3-1/2 cups confectioners' sugar
     1 teaspoon vanilla extract
Toasted chopped pecans

In a mixing bowl, cream butter and sugar. Add the eggs, one at a time, beating well after each addition. Beat in bananas and vanilla. Combine dry ingredients; add to creamed mixture alternately with buttermilk. Stir in pecans. Pour into three greased and floured 9-in. round baking pans. Bake at 350° for 30-35 minutes or until a toothpick inserted near the center comes out clean. Cool for 10 minutes before removing from pans to wire racks to cool completely.

For frosting, beat cream cheese, butter and sugar in a small mixing bowl. Add vanilla. Spread between layers and on top of cake. Sprinkle with pecans. Store in the refrigerator. **Yield:** 12-16 servings.

Layered Chocolate Cake

Dorothy Monroe, Pocatello, Idaho

(Pictured above)

It is hard to believe this impressive dessert starts with a boxed cake mix. Cream cheese in the icing provides the luscious finishing touch.

     1 package (18-1/4 ounces) German chocolate
          cake mix
1-1/3 cups water
     3 eggs
     1/3 cup vegetable oil
     1 package (3 ounces) cook-and-serve vanilla
          pudding mix
     1 teaspoon unflavored gelatin
     2 cups milk
     1 package (8 ounces) cream cheese, softened
     1/2 cup butter *or* margarine, softened
     1 teaspoon vanilla extract
1-1/2 cups confectioners' sugar
     3 tablespoons baking cocoa

In a mixing bowl, combine the first four ingredients; mix well. Pour into a greased 15-in. x 10-in. x 1-in. baking pan. Bake at 350° for 23-25 minutes. Cool on a wire rack. In a saucepan, combine pudding mix, gelatin and milk; cook according to package directions for pudding. Cool.

Cut cake into three 10-in. x 5-in. rectangles. Place one on a serving platter. Spread with half of the pudding mixture; repeat layers. Top with third layer. In a mixing bowl, beat cream cheese and butter. Add vanilla; mix well. Add sugar and cocoa; beat until smooth. Frost top and sides of cake. Store in the refrigerator. **Yield:** 10 servings.

Zucchini Fudge Cake

Robert Keith, Rochester, Minnesota

My garden produces a bumper crop of zucchini each year, and I hate to see even one go to waste. This scrumptious cake puts that plentiful produce to great use!

     1 cup butter *or* margarine, softened
2-1/2 cups sugar
     4 eggs
     2 teaspoons vanilla extract
     3 cups all-purpose flour
     1/2 cup baking cocoa
     2 teaspoons baking powder
     1 teaspoon baking soda
     3/4 teaspoon salt
     1 cup buttermilk
     3 cups shredded zucchini
3-1/2 cups prepared chocolate frosting

In a mixing bowl, cream butter and sugar. Add eggs, one at a time, beating well after each addition. Beat in vanilla. Combine flour, cocoa, baking powder, baking soda and salt; add to the creamed mixture alternately with buttermilk. Stir in zucchini.

Pour into three greased and floured 9-in. round baking pans. Bake at 350° for 25-30 minutes or until a toothpick inserted near the center comes out clean. Cool for 10 minutes before removing from pans to wire racks to cool completely. Frost between layers and top and sides of cake. **Yield:** 12-14 servings.

p. 49

p. 47

p. 53

p. 52

p. 44

Clockwise from top left: Cherry Chocolate Marble Cake, Cinnamon Nut Cake, Old-Fashioned Raisin Cake, Surprise Carrot Cake and Caramel Apple Cake.

Tube Cakes

Caramel Apple Cake

Marilyn Paradis, Woodburn, Oregon

(Pictured below and on page 42)

When I go to potlucks, family gatherings or on hunting and fishing trips with my husband and son, this cake is one of my favorite desserts to bring. The flavorful cake stays moist as long as it lasts, which isn't long!

1-1/2 cups vegetable oil
1-1/2 cups sugar
  1/2 cup packed brown sugar
    3 eggs
    3 cups all-purpose flour
    2 teaspoons ground cinnamon
  1/2 teaspoon ground nutmeg
    1 teaspoon baking soda
  1/2 teaspoon salt
3-1/2 cups diced peeled apples
    1 cup chopped walnuts
    2 teaspoons vanilla extract
CARAMEL ICING:
  1/2 cup packed brown sugar
  1/3 cup half-and-half cream
  1/4 cup butter *or* margarine
Dash salt
    1 cup confectioners' sugar
Chopped walnuts, optional

In a mixing bowl, combine oil and sugars. Add eggs, one at a time, beating well after each addition. Combine dry ingredients; add to batter and stir well. Fold in apples, walnuts and vanilla. Pour into a greased and floured 10-in. tube pan. Bake at 325° for 1-1/2 hours or until a toothpick inserted near the center comes out clean. Cool for 10 minutes before removing from pan to a wire rack to cool completely.

In the top of a double boiler over simmering water, heat brown sugar, cream, butter and salt until sugar is dissolved. Cool to room temperature. Beat in confectioners' sugar until smooth; drizzle over cake. Sprinkle with nuts if desired. **Yield:** 12-16 servings.

Blueberry Oat Cake

Linda Police, Dover, New Jersey

(Pictured above)

This is my favorite blueberry recipe. Everyone in my family likes it, so I make it rather frequently. It's moist, nutritious and very easy to make.

    2 eggs
    2 cups buttermilk
    1 cup packed brown sugar
  1/2 cup vegetable oil
    2 cups all-purpose flour
    2 teaspoons baking powder
    1 teaspoon baking soda
    1 teaspoon ground cinnamon
  1/2 teaspoon salt
    2 cups quick-cooking oats
    2 cups fresh *or* frozen blueberries*
    1 cup chopped walnuts, optional
Confectioners' sugar

In a mixing bowl, beat the eggs, buttermilk, brown sugar and oil. Combine the flour, baking powder, baking soda, cinnamon and salt; add to batter. Beat on low speed for 2 minutes. Fold in oats, blueberries and walnuts if desired. Transfer to a greased and floured 10-in. fluted tube pan. Bake at 375° for 45-50 minutes or until a toothpick comes out clean. Cool for 10 minutes before removing from pan to a wire rack to cool completely. Dust with confectioners' sugar. **Yield:** 12-16 servings.

*Editor's Note: If using frozen blueberries, do not thaw them before adding to batter.

Nutmeg Pear Cake

Kim Rubner, Worthington, Iowa

I've been in love with baking since I was in seventh grade. I especially enjoy making this pear cake for my

husband and our two children. With its yummy apple cider sauce, it tastes like autumn.

3 cups all-purpose flour
1-1/2 teaspoons ground nutmeg
1 teaspoon baking soda
1 teaspoon ground cinnamon
3/4 teaspoon salt
1/2 teaspoon baking powder
2 cups sugar
1 cup vegetable oil
3 eggs, beaten
1/2 cup apple cider
3 teaspoons vanilla extract
1 can (29 ounces) pear halves, drained and mashed
1 cup chopped pecans

APPLE CIDER SAUCE:
3/4 cup butter *or* margarine
2/3 cup sugar
1/3 cup packed brown sugar
2 tablespoons cornstarch
2/3 cup apple cider
1/3 cup whipping cream
1/3 cup lemon juice

In a large bowl, combine the first six ingredients. In another bowl, whisk the sugar, oil, eggs, cider and vanilla. Add to the dry ingredients and stir well. Stir in pears and pecans. Pour into a greased and floured 10-in. fluted tube pan. Bake at 350° for 65-70 minutes or until a toothpick comes out clean. Cool for 10 minutes before removing from pan to a wire rack to cool completely.

For sauce, combine butter and sugars in a saucepan. Cook over low heat for 2-3 minutes or until sugar is dissolved. Combine the cornstarch and cider until smooth; add to sugar mixture. Stir in the cream and

lemon juice. Bring to a boil; cook and stir for 1-2 minutes or until thickened. Serve warm with cake. **Yield:** 12-15 servings.

Pineapple Bundt Cake

Fayne Lutz, Taos, New Mexico

(Pictured below)

Fruity and firm-textured, this beautiful cake is sure to impress. Bits of pineapple are in every bite.

1 cup butter *or* margarine, softened
1-1/2 cups sugar
2 eggs, lightly beaten
2 egg whites
2 teaspoons lemon extract
2-2/3 cups all-purpose flour
1 teaspoon baking powder
1 can (8 ounces) crushed pineapple, undrained

GLAZE:
1 cup confectioners' sugar
1 to 2 tablespoons milk
1/2 teaspoon lemon extract

In a mixing bowl, cream butter and sugar. Add eggs, egg whites and extract; beat until fluffy, about 2 minutes. Combine flour and baking powder; gradually add to creamed mixture. Stir in pineapple. Pour into a greased and floured 10-in. fluted bundt pan.

Bake at 350° for 55-60 minutes or until a toothpick comes out clean. Cool for 10 minutes before removing from pan to a wire rack to cool completely. In a small bowl, combine glaze ingredients until smooth. Drizzle over cake. **Yield:** 12-16 servings.

Banana Nut Cake

Gloria Barkley, Wilmington, North Carolina

(Pictured above)

I'm a pastor's wife and it's so good to have something to serve when friends drop in unexpectedly. Because this cake can be frozen and also keeps well in the refrigerator, I try to have one on hand…just in case.

>   3 cups all-purpose flour
>   2 cups sugar
>   1 teaspoon *each* baking powder, baking soda, salt, ground cinnamon and nutmeg
>   4 eggs, lightly beaten
> 1-1/3 cups vegetable oil
> 1-1/2 teaspoons vanilla extract
>   1 can (8 ounces) crushed pineapple, undrained
>   2 cups mashed ripe bananas (3 to 4 medium)
> 1-1/2 cups chopped walnuts
> Confectioners' sugar

In a mixing bowl, combine dry ingredients. Beat in eggs, oil and vanilla. Fold in pineapple, bananas and nuts. Pour into a greased and floured 10-in. tube pan. Bake at 350° for 60-65 minutes or until a toothpick comes out clean. Cool for 15 minutes before removing from pan to a wire rack to cool completely. Dust with confectioners' sugar. **Yield:** 12-16 servings.

Chocolate Sweet Potato Cake

Sally Green, Mobile, Alabama

This recipe was given to my mother in 1940. Mother had lost all of her recipes, collected during 7 years of marriage, in a house fire, so her friends gave her a recipe party. Among those recipes was this cake, which has become one of our family's favorites. The flavors of chocolate and sweet potato really complement each other.

> 2/3 cup butter *or* margarine, softened
>   2 cups sugar
>   4 eggs
>   2 cups all-purpose flour
>   1 tablespoon baking cocoa
>   1 teaspoon baking soda
>   1 teaspoon baking powder
>   1 teaspoon *each* ground cinnamon, nutmeg, allspice and cloves
> 1/2 cup milk
>   2 medium sweet potatoes, peeled, cooked, mashed and cooled
>   1 teaspoon vanilla extract
>   2 cups chopped pecans

1/2 cup raisins
Confectioners' sugar, optional

In a mixing bowl, cream butter and sugar. Add eggs, one at a time, beating well after each addition. Combine the dry ingredients; add to creamed mixture alternately with milk. Stir in sweet potatoes and vanilla; mix well. Add the pecans and raisins. Transfer to a greased and floured 10-in. fluted tube pan.

Bake at 350° for 70-80 minutes or until a toothpick inserted near the center comes out clean. Cool for 10 minutes before removing from pan to a wire rack to cool completely. Dust with confectioners' sugar if desired. **Yield:** 12-16 servings.

Cinnamon Nut Cake

Margaret Wilson, Hemet, California

(Pictured below and on page 42)

This moist bundt cake is an easy-to-assemble treat for brunch or dessert. Top with a dollop of whipped cream and you're ready to enjoy.

    1 package (18-1/4 ounces) yellow cake mix
    3 eggs
1-1/3 cups water
    1/4 cup vegetable oil
1-1/4 cups finely chopped walnuts
7-1/2 teaspoons sugar
4-1/2 teaspoons ground cinnamon

In a mixing bowl, combine the cake mix, eggs, water and oil. Beat on medium speed for 2 minutes. Combine walnuts, sugar and cinnamon. Sprinkle a third of the nut mixture into a greased and floured 10-in. fluted tube pan. Top with half of the batter and another third of the nut mixture. Repeat layers.

Bake at 350° for 35-40 minutes or until a toothpick inserted near the center comes out clean. Cool for 10 minutes before removing from pan to a wire rack to cool completely. **Yield:** 12-14 servings.

Cranberry Bundt Cake

Esther McCoy, Dillonvale, Ohio

(Pictured above)

The first time I served this cake was at Thanksgiving dinner several years ago. Along with pumpkin pies, it's become our traditional annual holiday dessert. It's festive and very flavorful.

    2/3 cup butter *or* margarine, softened
    1 cup sugar
    3 eggs
1-1/2 teaspoons vanilla extract
    2 cups all-purpose flour
    1 teaspoon baking powder
    3/4 teaspoon baking soda
    1/2 teaspoon salt
    1 cup (8 ounces) sour cream
    3/4 cup chopped dried cranberries
    1/3 cup chopped pecans
Confectioners' sugar

In a mixing bowl, cream butter and sugar. Add the eggs, one at a time, beating well after each addition. Stir in the vanilla. Combine the flour, baking powder, baking soda and salt; add to the creamed mixture alternately with sour cream. Fold in the cranberries and pecans. Pour into a greased and floured 8-in. fluted tube pan.

Bake at 350° for 45-50 minutes or until a toothpick inserted near the center comes out clean. Cool for 10 minutes; remove from pan to a wire rack to cool completely. Dust with confectioners' sugar. **Yield:** 8-10 servings.

Editor's Note: Cake can be baked in a 9-in. square baking pan at the same time and temperature.

Chocolate Potato Cake

Charlotte Cleveland, Hobbs, New Mexico

(Pictured above)

This scrumptious cake recipe has been handed down for generations in my family.

  1 cup butter-flavored shortening
  2 cups sugar
  2 eggs, *separated*
  1 cup mashed potatoes
  1 teaspoon vanilla extract
2-1/2 cups all-purpose flour
  1/2 cup baking cocoa
2-1/2 teaspoons baking powder
  3/4 teaspoon salt
  1/2 teaspoon *each* ground allspice, cinnamon,
    cloves and nutmeg
  1 cup milk
MOCHA FROSTING:
  1/3 cup butter *or* margarine, softened
2-2/3 cups confectioners' sugar
  2 tablespoons baking cocoa
  1/4 teaspoon salt
  3 tablespoons strong brewed coffee

In a mixing bowl, cream shortening and sugar. Add the egg yolks, one at a time, beating well after each addition. Add potatoes and vanilla; mix well. Combine the dry ingredients; add to the creamed mixture alternately with milk. In a small mixing bowl, beat egg whites until soft peaks form; fold into batter. Pour into a greased and floured 10-in. fluted tube pan.

Bake at 325° for 1 to 1-1/4 hours or until a toothpick inserted near the center comes out clean. Cool for 10 minutes before removing from pan to a wire rack to cool completely. In a small bowl, combine frosting ingredients until smooth. Frost cake. **Yield:** 16 servings.

Pecan Carrot Bundt Cake

Joan Taylor, Adrian, Minnesota

(Pictured below)

The pecans and citrus flavor make this dessert special. I use fresh carrots from my garden.

  1 cup butter *or* margarine, softened
  1 cup sugar
  1 cup packed brown sugar
  4 eggs
  2 tablespoons grated lemon peel
  2 tablespoons grated orange peel
  3 cups all-purpose flour
  2 teaspoons baking powder
  1 teaspoon baking soda
  1 teaspoon ground cinnamon
  1/2 teaspoon salt
  2 tablespoons orange juice
  2 tablespoons lemon juice
  1 pound carrots, grated
  1 cup raisins
  1 cup chopped pecans
FROSTING:
  1 package (3 ounces) cream cheese, softened
1-1/2 to 2 cups confectioners' sugar
  1 teaspoon vanilla extract
  1/2 cup chopped pecans

In a mixing bowl, cream butter and sugars. Add eggs, one at a time, beating well after each. Beat in lemon and orange peels. Combine dry ingredients; gradually add to creamed mixture alternately with juices. Stir in carrots, raisins and pecans. Pour into a greased and floured 10-in. fluted tube pan.

Bake at 350° for 50-60 minutes or until a toothpick comes out clean. Cool for 10 minutes; remove from pan to a wire rack. In a mixing bowl, beat the cream cheese, confectioners' sugar and vanilla until smooth. Frost cake; sprinkle with pecans. Store in the refrigerator. **Yield:** 12-16 servings.

Beet Bundt Cake

Vermadel Kirby, Milford, Delaware

I found this recipe handwritten in my grandmother's well-worn cookbook. I've made it many times.

    1 cup butter *or* margarine, softened, *divided*
1-1/2 cups packed dark brown sugar
    3 eggs
    4 squares (1 ounce *each*) semisweet
       chocolate
    2 cups pureed cooked beets
    1 teaspoon vanilla extract
    2 cups all-purpose flour
    2 teaspoons baking soda
    1/4 teaspoon salt
Confectioners' sugar

In a mixing bowl, cream 3/4 cup butter and brown sugar. Add eggs; mix well. Melt chocolate with remaining butter; stir until smooth. Cool slightly. Blend chocolate mixture, beets and vanilla into the creamed mixture (mixture will appear separated). Combine flour, baking soda and salt; add to the creamed mixture and mix well. Pour into a greased and floured 10-in. fluted tube pan.

Bake at 375° for 45-55 minutes or until a toothpick inserted near the center comes out clean. Cool in pan 10 minutes before removing to a wire rack to cool completely. Dust with confectioners' sugar. **Yield:** 16-20 servings.

Rice Pudding Cake

Nancy Horsburgh, Everett, Ontario

The secret ingredient in this delicious cake is rice. It tastes a lot like rice pudding, only in a different form.

    1/2 cup raisins
Boiling water
    1 cup uncooked long grain rice
    1 quart milk
    3/4 cup butter *or* margarine, softened
    1 cup sugar
    5 eggs, *separated*
    2 tablespoons grated orange peel
    2 tablespoons graham cracker crumbs
Confectioners' sugar

In a bowl, cover raisins with boiling water. Let stand 5 minutes; drain and set aside. In a large saucepan, cover rice with water; bring to a boil. Drain the liquid; add milk to rice. Bring to a boil. Reduce heat; cover and simmer for 15-20 minutes or until rice is tender.

In a mixing bowl, cream butter and sugar. Add egg yolks; beat well. Add rice mixture, raisins and orange peel. Beat the egg whites until stiff; fold into the batter. Spoon into a greased 10-in. tube pan. Sprinkle with crumbs. Bake at 350° for 55-60 minutes or until set. Cool in pan for 20 minutes. Loosen sides and center with a knife. Carefully invert onto a serving plate. Dust with confectioners' sugar. Serve warm or chilled. **Yield:** 12-16 servings.

Cherry Chocolate Marble Cake

Sandra Campbell, Chase Mills, New York

(Pictured above and on page 42)

I got this recipe from one of my husband's co-workers. It's now a favorite of our family and friends.

    1 cup butter *or* margarine, softened
    2 cups sugar
    3 eggs
    6 tablespoons maraschino cherry juice
    6 tablespoons water
    1 teaspoon almond extract
3-3/4 cups all-purpose flour
2-1/4 teaspoons baking soda
    3/4 teaspoon salt
1-1/2 cups (12 ounces) sour cream
    3/4 cup chopped maraschino cherries, drained
    3/4 cup chopped walnuts, toasted
    3 squares (1 ounce *each*) unsweetened
       chocolate, melted
Confectioners' sugar

In a mixing bowl, cream butter and sugar. Add the eggs, one at a time, beating well after each addition. Add the cherry juice, water and extract; mix well. Combine flour, baking soda and salt; add to creamed mixture alternately with sour cream. Mix just until combined.

Divide batter in half. To one portion, add cherries and walnuts; mix well. To the second portion, add chocolate; mix well. Spoon half of the cherry mixture into a greased and floured 10-in. fluted tube pan. Cover with half of the chocolate mixture. Repeat layers.

Bake at 350° for 1 hour and 15 minutes or until a toothpick inserted near the center comes out clean. Cool for 15 minutes before removing from pan to a wire rack to cool completely. Dust with confectioners' sugar. **Yield:** 10-12 servings.

Chocolate Yum-Yum Cake

Dorothy Colli, West Hartford, Connecticut

(Pictured below)

My grandmother first made this cake, and my mother made it often when I was a little girl. Today, I'm still baking it. What better testimony to a delicious recipe! You can frost it or just sprinkle it with a little powdered sugar. Either way, it's great.

```
    1/2 cup butter (no substitutes)
      2 squares (1 ounce each) unsweetened
        baking chocolate
      1 cup sugar
    1/2 cup raisins
  1-1/2 cups water
    1/2 teaspoon ground cinnamon
    1/4 teaspoon ground cloves
Pinch salt
  1-1/2 teaspoons vanilla extract
  1-3/4 cups all-purpose flour
      1 teaspoon baking soda
ICING:
    1/2 cup confectioners' sugar
    1/4 teaspoon vanilla extract
      1 to 2 teaspoons milk
```

In a large saucepan over low heat, melt butter and chocolate, stirring constantly. Add sugar, raisins, water, cinnamon and cloves; bring to a boil. Boil for 5 minutes, stirring occasionally. Remove from the heat; pour into a mixing bowl and cool for 15 minutes. Add salt and vanilla. Combine flour and baking soda; add to chocolate mixture and mix well. Pour into a greased and floured 8-cup fluted tube pan.

Bake at 350° for 45 minutes or until a toothpick inserted near the center comes out clean. Cool for 10 minutes before removing from pan to a wire rack to cool completely. Combine icing ingredients; spoon over cake. **Yield:** 8-10 servings.

Editor's Note: An 11-in. x 7-in. x 2-in. baking pan can be used. Bake for 25-30 minutes or until cake tests done.

Sugar Plum Cake

Mark Brown, Birmingham, Alabama

I came by my love of preparing recipes as a boy in the South, where food is the center of every gathering. I worked with my grandmothers, who believed everyone should know how to cook. This cake recipe is a favorite. I bake several for Christmas each year to give as gifts.

```
      2 cups self-rising flour*
      2 cups sugar
      1 teaspoon ground cinnamon
      1 teaspoon ground cloves
    3/4 cup vegetable oil
      2 jars (6 ounces each) strained plum baby food
      3 eggs, beaten
      1 cup chopped pecans
```

GLAZE:
  1 cup plus 2 tablespoons confectioners' sugar
  1 jar (4 ounces) strained plum-apple baby food
  2 tablespoons milk

In a large bowl, combine flour, sugar, cinnamon and cloves. Stir in oil, baby food and eggs. Fold in pecans. Pour into a greased and floured 10-in. tube pan. Bake at 350° for 50-60 minutes or until a toothpick inserted near the center comes out clean. Cool for 10 minutes before removing from pan to a wire rack to cool completely.

In a small bowl, combine glaze ingredients until smooth. Drizzle over top and sides of cake. **Yield:** 16-20 servings.

*Editors Note: As a substitute for each cup of self-rising flour, place 1-1/2 teaspoons baking powder and 1/2 teaspoon salt in a measuring cup. Add all-purpose flour to measure 1 cup.

Prune Bundt Cake

Gina Mueller, Converse, Texas

(Pictured above)

Moist, flavorful and simply scrumptious, this old-fashioned cake was one of my mom's best desserts. Top it with confectioners' sugar or frosting for a sweet treat sure to win raves.

  1/2 cup butter-flavored shortening
  1 cup sugar
  2 eggs
  2 cups all-purpose flour
  1 teaspoon baking soda
  1 teaspoon ground cinnamon
  3/4 teaspoon salt

  1/4 teaspoon *each* ground allspice, cloves and nutmeg
  1 cup prune juice
  1 cup finely chopped prunes
Confectioners' sugar, optional

In a mixing bowl, cream shortening and sugar until light and fluffy. Add eggs, one at a time, beating well after each addition. Combine the dry ingredients; add to creamed mixture alternately with prune juice. Stir in prunes. Pour into a greased and floured 10-in. fluted tube pan.

Bake at 350° for 40-45 minutes or until a toothpick comes out clean. Cool for 10 minutes before removing from pan to a wire rack to cool completely. Dust with confectioners' sugar if desired. **Yield:** 12 servings.

Poppy Seed Bundt Cake

Kathy Schrecengost, Oswego, New York

(Pictured below)

This cake tastes so good, you might be tempted not to tell anyone it starts with a mix! A hint of coconut and the tender texture make it simply scrumptious.

  1 package (18-1/4 ounces) yellow cake mix
  1 package (3.4 ounces) instant coconut cream pudding mix
  1 cup water
  1/2 cup vegetable oil
  3 eggs
  2 tablespoons poppy seeds
Confectioners' sugar

In a mixing bowl, combine cake and pudding mixes, water, oil and eggs. Beat on low speed until moistened. Beat on medium for 2 minutes. Stir in the poppy seeds. Pour into a greased and floured 10-in. fluted tube pan.

Bake at 350° for 48-52 minutes or until a toothpick inserted near the center comes out clean. Cool for 10 minutes before removing from pan to a wire rack to cool completely. Dust with confectioners' sugar. **Yield:** 12-15 servings.

Surprise Carrot Cake

Lisa Bowen, Little Britain, Ontario

(Pictured above and on page 42)

A cousin gave me this recipe. It's a wonderful potluck pleaser with its "surprise" cream cheese center. My husband and our two young children love it, too! It's a great way to use up the overabundance of carrots from my vegetable garden.

> 3 eggs
> 1-3/4 cups sugar
> 3 cups shredded carrots
> 1 cup vegetable oil
> 2 cups all-purpose flour
> 2 teaspoons baking soda
> 2 teaspoons ground cinnamon
> 1 teaspoon salt
> 1/2 cup chopped pecans
> FILLING:
> 1 package (8 ounces) cream cheese, softened
> 1/4 cup sugar
> 1 egg
> FROSTING:
> 1 package (8 ounces) cream cheese, softened
> 1/4 cup butter *or* margarine, softened
> 2 teaspoons vanilla extract
> 4 cups confectioners' sugar

In a mixing bowl, beat eggs and sugar. Add carrots and oil; beat until blended. Combine the flour, baking soda, cinnamon and salt. Add to carrot mixture; mix well. Stir in pecans. Pour 3 cups batter into a greased and floured 10-in. fluted tube pan. In a mixing bowl, beat cream cheese and sugar. Add egg; mix well. Spoon over batter. Top with remaining batter.

Bake at 350° for 55-60 minutes or until a toothpick in-serted near the center comes out clean. Cool for 10 minutes before removing from pan to a wire rack to cool completely.

For frosting, in a small mixing bowl, beat the cream cheese, butter and vanilla until smooth. Gradually add confectioners' sugar. Frost cake. Store in the refrigerator. **Yield:** 12-16 servings.

Cranberry Sauce Cake

Marge Clark, West Lebanon, Indiana

(Pictured below)

This moist cake is so easy to make because it mixes in one bowl. Slice it at the table so everyone can see how beautiful it is. Make one for your dinner and another for a friend.

> 3 cups all-purpose flour
> 1-1/2 cups sugar
> 1 cup mayonnaise
> 1 can (16 ounces) whole-berry cranberry sauce
> 1/3 cup orange juice
> 1 tablespoon grated orange peel
> 1 teaspoon baking soda
> 1 teaspoon salt
> 1 teaspoon orange extract
> 1 cup chopped walnuts
> ICING:
> 1 cup confectioners' sugar
> 1 to 2 tablespoons orange juice

In a mixing bowl, combine flour, sugar, mayonnaise, cranberry sauce, orange juice and peel, baking soda, salt and extract; mix well. Fold in walnuts. Cut waxed or parchment paper to fit the bottom of a 10-in. tube pan. Spray the pan and paper with nonstick cooking spray. Pour batter into paper-lined pan.

Bake at 350° for 60-70 minutes or until a toothpick in-serted near the center comes out clean. Cool for 10 minutes before removing from pan to a wire rack. Combine icing ingredients; drizzle over the warm cake. **Yield:** 12-16 servings.

Milk Chocolate Bundt Cake

Sharan Williams, Spanish Fork, Utah

Try this recipe for a moist mild chocolate cake that cuts cleanly and doesn't need frosting. This scrumptious snack cake travels very well.

     1 milk chocolate candy bar (7 ounces)
 1/2 cup chocolate syrup
     1 cup butter *or* margarine, softened
 1-1/2 cups sugar
     4 eggs
     1 teaspoon vanilla extract
 2-3/4 cups all-purpose flour
 1/2 teaspoon salt
 1/2 teaspoon baking soda
     1 cup buttermilk
Confectioners' sugar

In a saucepan, heat the candy bar and chocolate syrup over low heat until melted; set aside to cool. In a mixing bowl, cream butter and sugar. Add eggs, one at a time, beating well after each addition. Stir in chocolate mixture and vanilla. Combine flour, salt and baking soda; add to creamed mixture alternately with buttermilk. Pour into a greased and floured 10-in. fluted tube pan.

Bake at 350° for 65-70 minutes or until a toothpick comes out clean. Cool for 15 minutes before removing from pan to a wire rack to cool completely. Dust with confectioners' sugar. **Yield:** 12-14 servings.

Old-Fashioned Raisin Cake

Norma Poole, Auburndale, Florida

(Pictured above and on page 42)

This is a wonderful cake for the holidays. It fills the house with a heavenly aroma when it's baking.

     1 large navel orange, cut into 8 wedges
     1 cup raisins
 1/2 cup pecans
 1/2 cup butter *or* margarine, softened
     1 cup sugar
     2 eggs
     1 teaspoon vanilla extract
     2 cups all-purpose flour
     1 teaspoon baking soda
 1/2 teaspoon salt
 2/3 cup buttermilk
GLAZE:
 1/2 cup confectioners' sugar
     2 tablespoons orange juice

In a food processor, combine the orange, raisins and pecans. Cover and process until mixture is finely chopped; set aside. In a mixing bowl, cream butter and sugar. Beat in eggs and vanilla; mix well. Combine the flour, baking soda and salt; add to creamed mixture alternately with buttermilk. Stir in orange mixture. Pour into a greased and floured 10-in. fluted tube pan.

Bake at 325° for 45-55 minutes or until a toothpick inserted near the center comes out clean. Cool for 10 minutes; invert onto a wire rack. In a small bowl, combine glaze ingredients until smooth; brush over warm cake. Cool completely before serving. **Yield:** 10-12 servings.

p. 57

p. 61

p. 60

p. 56

p. 58

Clockwise from top left: Holiday Pound Cake, Chocolate Berry Pound Cake, Sesame Pound Cake, Orange Date Pound Cake and White Chocolate Pound Cake.

Pound Cakes

Cranberry-Orange Pound Cake

Sheree Swistun, Winnipeg, Manitoba

(Pictured above)

At the summer tourist resort in Ontario my husband and I operate, we prepare all the meals for our guests. I'm always trying out new recipes. This one's a keeper.

1-1/2 cups butter (no substitutes), softened
2-3/4 cups sugar
   6 eggs
   1 teaspoon vanilla extract
2-1/2 teaspoons grated orange peel
   3 cups all-purpose flour
   1 teaspoon baking powder
  1/2 teaspoon salt
   1 cup (8 ounces) sour cream
1-1/2 cups chopped fresh *or* frozen cranberries
VANILLA BUTTER SAUCE:
   1 cup sugar
   1 tablespoon all-purpose flour
  1/2 cup half-and-half cream
  1/2 cup butter, softened
  1/2 teaspoon vanilla extract

In a mixing bowl, cream butter. Gradually beat in sugar until light and fluffy, about 5-7 minutes. Add eggs, one at a time, beating well after each. Stir in vanilla and orange peel. Combine flour, baking powder and salt; add to creamed mixture alternately with sour cream. Beat on low just until blended. Fold in cranberries. Pour into a greased and floured 10-in. fluted tube pan.

Bake at 350° for 65-70 minutes or until a toothpick inserted near the center comes out clean. Cool for 10 minutes before removing from pan to a wire rack to cool completely. In a small saucepan, combine sugar and flour. Stir in cream and butter; bring to a boil over medium heat, stirring constantly. Boil for 2 minutes. Remove from the heat and stir in vanilla. Serve warm over cake. **Yield:** 16 servings (1-1/2 cups sauce).

Caramel Pecan Pound Cake

Rosella Day, Waycross, Georgia

My state is known for the delicious pecans it produces, so this recipe definitely represents Georgia. The pecan flavor comes through nicely in this cake.

   1 cup butter (no substitutes), softened
2-1/4 cups packed brown sugar
   1 cup sugar
   5 eggs
   3 teaspoons vanilla extract
   3 cups all-purpose flour
  1/2 teaspoon baking powder
  1/2 teaspoon salt
   1 cup milk
   1 cup finely chopped pecans
Confectioners' sugar
Fresh fruit, optional

In a mixing bowl, cream butter. Gradually beat in sugars until light and fluffy. Add eggs, one at a time, beating well after each. Stir in vanilla. Combine the flour, baking powder and salt; add to the creamed mixture alternately with milk. Beat on low speed just until blended. Fold in pecans. Pour into a greased and floured 10-in. tube pan.

Bake at 325° for 1-1/2 hours or until a toothpick inserted near the center comes out clean. Cool for 10 minutes before removing from pan to a wire rack to cool completely. Dust with confectioners' sugar. Serve with fruit if desired. **Yield:** 16 servings.

Orange Date Pound Cake

Ruth Bartz, Suring, Wisconsin

(Pictured below and on page 54)

Loaded with chewy dates and crunchy pecans, this cake is a "must" to take to family gatherings. The sweet and zesty orange sauce tops it off just right. This cake slices nicely and looks so appetizing served on a pretty plate.

1 cup butter *or* margarine, softened
3 cups sugar, *divided*
4 eggs
1 tablespoon orange peel, *divided*
3 cups all-purpose flour
1 teaspoon baking soda
1-1/3 cups buttermilk
1 pound chopped dates
1 cup coarsely chopped pecans
1/2 cup orange juice

In a mixing bowl, cream butter and 2 cups sugar. Add the eggs, one at a time, beating well after each addition. Add 2 teaspoons orange peel. Combine flour and baking soda; add to the creamed mixture alternately with buttermilk. Stir in dates and pecans. Pour into a greased and floured 10-in. tube pan; spread evenly.

Bake at 325° for 70-75 minutes or until a toothpick comes out clean. Combine the orange juice and remaining sugar and orange peel; pour over cake. Cool for 30 minutes before removing from pan to a wire rack to cool completely. **Yield:** 12-16 servings.

Eggnog Pound Cake

Theresa Koetter, Borden, Indiana

A flavorful blend of eggnog and nutmeg makes this cake a natural holiday favorite.

1 package (18-1/4 ounces) yellow cake mix
1 cup eggnog*
3 eggs
1/2 cup butter *or* margarine, softened
1/2 to 1 teaspoon ground nutmeg
CUSTARD SAUCE:
1/4 cup sugar
1 tablespoon cornstarch
1/4 teaspoon salt
1 cup milk
1 egg yolk, lightly beaten
1 teaspoon butter *or* margarine
1 teaspoon vanilla extract
1/2 cup whipping cream, whipped

In a mixing bowl, combine the first five ingredients. Beat on low until moistened, scraping bowl occasionally. Beat on medium for 2 minutes. Pour into a greased and floured 12-cup fluted tube pan. Bake at 350° for 40-45 minutes or until a toothpick inserted near the center comes out clean. Cool for 10 minutes before removing from pan to a wire rack to cool completely.

For sauce, combine sugar, cornstarch and salt in a saucepan; gradually stir in milk. Bring to a boil over medium heat; boil for 1-2 minutes, stirring constantly. Blend a small amount into egg yolk. Return all to the pan; mix well. Cook and stir for 2 minutes. Remove from the heat; stir in butter and vanilla. Cool for 15 minutes. Fold in whipped cream. Store in the refrigerator. Serve with the cake. **Yield:** 16-20 servings.

***Editor's Note:** This recipe was tested with commercially prepared eggnog.*

Holiday Pound Cake

Ruby Williams, Bogalusa, Louisiana

(Pictured above and on page 54)

We top off our Thanksgiving feast with this mellow, tender cake dressed up with a strawberry topping. Pound cake is a Southern tradition, and I'm proud to say I've baked hundreds of them over the years. It's a pleasure to share my recipe.

1 cup butter (no substitutes), softened
1/2 cup shortening
1 package (3 ounces) cream cheese, softened
2-1/2 cups sugar
5 eggs
3 cups cake flour
1 teaspoon baking powder
1/2 teaspoon salt
1 cup buttermilk
1 teaspoon lemon extract
1 teaspoon vanilla extract
Strawberry ice cream topping
Sliced fresh strawberries, optional

In a large mixing bowl, cream butter, shortening and cream cheese. Gradually add sugar, beating until light and fluffy. Add eggs, one at a time, beating well after each. Combine the dry ingredients; add to creamed mixture alternately with buttermilk. Stir in extracts. Pour into a greased and floured 10-in. fluted tube pan.

Bake at 325° for 1 hour and 20 minutes or until a toothpick inserted near the center comes out clean. Cool for 10 minutes before removing from pan to a wire rack to cool completely. Serve with strawberry topping and fresh strawberries if desired. **Yield:** 12-16 servings.

White Chocolate Pound Cake

Kimberley Thompson, Fayetteville, Georgia

(Pictured below and on page 54)

I often bake this moist bundt cake, drizzled with two types of chocolate glaze, for special occasions.

- 8 squares (1 ounce *each*) white baking chocolate
- 1 cup butter (no substitutes), softened
- 2 cups plus 2 tablespoons sugar, *divided*
- 5 eggs
- 2 teaspoons vanilla extract
- 1/2 teaspoon almond extract
- 3 cups all-purpose flour
- 1 teaspoon baking powder
- 1/2 teaspoon salt
- 1/4 teaspoon baking soda
- 1 cup (8 ounces) sour cream

GLAZE:
- 4 squares (1 ounce *each*) semisweet baking chocolate, melted
- 4 squares (1 ounce *each*) white baking chocolate, melted

Whole fresh strawberries, optional

Chop four squares of white chocolate and melt the other four; set both aside. In a mixing bowl, cream butter and 2 cups sugar until light and fluffy, about 5 minutes. Add eggs, one at a time, beating well after each addition. Stir in extracts and the melted chocolate. Combine flour, baking powder, salt and baking soda; add to the creamed mixture alternately with sour cream. Beat just until combined.

Grease a 10-in. fluted tube pan. Sprinkle with the remaining sugar. Pour a third of the batter into pan. Sprinkle with half of the chopped chocolate. Repeat. Pour remaining batter on top. Bake at 350° for 55-60 minutes or until a toothpick inserted near the center comes out clean. Cool for 10 minutes; remove from pan to a wire rack to cool completely. Drizzle semisweet and white chocolate over cake. Garnish with strawberries if desired. **Yield:** 16 servings.

Golden Lemon Pound Cake

Reverend Douglas Jenkins, Ottawa, Kansas

While pastoring a church in New Mexico, I worked in a nursing home. One day I baked this cake. Everyone raved over the treat "my wife made". When I told the residents I'd made it myself, they were astonished.

- 2/3 cup butter-flavored shortening
- 1-1/4 cups sugar
- 2 tablespoons lemon juice
- 1 teaspoon lemon extract
- 2/3 cup milk
- 2-1/4 cups cake flour
- 1-1/4 teaspoons salt
- 1 teaspoon baking powder
- 3 eggs

Confectioners' sugar

In a mixing bowl, cream shortening and sugar. Beat in lemon juice and extract. Add milk; beat for 30 seconds. Sift cake flour, salt and baking powder; gradually add to creamed mixture. Beat on low speed for 2 minutes. Add eggs, one at a time, beating for 1 minute after each.

Pour into a greased waxed paper-lined 9-in. x 5-in. x 3-in. loaf pan. Bake at 300° for 1 hour and 30 minutes or until a toothpick comes out clean. Cool for 10 minutes before removing from pan to a wire rack to cool completely. Remove waxed paper. Dust with confectioners' sugar. **Yield:** 1 loaf.

Blueberry-Peach Pound Cake

Nancy Zimmerman
Cape May Court House, New Jersey

(Pictured above)

I was going to make apple pound cake but found I had no apples. I had picked up blueberries and peaches from a local grower, so I decided to use them instead.

1/2 cup butter *or* margarine, softened
1-1/4 cups sugar
3 eggs
1/4 cup milk
2-1/2 cups cake flour
2 teaspoons baking powder
1/4 teaspoon salt
2-1/4 cups chopped peeled fresh peaches
(1/2-inch pieces)
2 cups fresh *or* frozen blueberries
Confectioners' sugar

In a mixing bowl, cream butter and sugar. Beat in eggs, one at a time. Beat in milk. Combine the flour, baking powder and salt; add to creamed mixture. Stir in peaches and blueberries. Pour into a greased and floured 10-in. fluted tube pan.

Bake at 350° for 60-70 minutes or until a toothpick comes out clean. Cool for 15 minutes before removing from pan to a wire rack to cool completely. Dust with confectioners' sugar. **Yield:** 10-12 servings.

Perfect Pound Cakes

FOR the best results when making pound cakes, let eggs stand at room temperature for 30 minutes before using in the recipe.

Cream Cheese Pound Cake

Mrs. Michael Ewanek, Hastings, Pennsylvania

(Pictured below)

I got this recipe from a woman who came to my rummage sale. We got to talking about zucchini and she didn't know what the big squash could be used for. So I sent her some of my favorite zucchini recipes and, in return, she mailed me the recipe for this cake. It's absolutely delicious and I've made it often.

1-1/2 cups butter (no substitutes), softened
1 package (8 ounces) cream cheese, softened
2-1/3 cups sugar
6 eggs
3 cups all-purpose flour
1 teaspoon vanilla extract

In a large mixing bowl, cream butter and cream cheese. Gradually add sugar, beating until light and fluffy, about 5-7 minutes. Add eggs, one at a time, beating well after each addition. Gradually add flour; beat just until blended. Stir in vanilla. Pour into a greased and floured 10-in. tube pan.

Bake at 300° for 1-1/2 hours or until a toothpick inserted near the center comes out clean. Cool for 15 minutes before removing from pan to a wire rack to cool completely. Store in the refrigerator. **Yield:** 12-16 servings.

Chocolate Chip Pound Cake

Michele Strunks, Brookville, Ohio

(Pictured below)

My mom has been making this cake for over 30 years. Dotted with chips and topped with a chocolate glaze, it is absolutely divine. I once got up at 5 a.m. to bake a cake before work so the ladies in my office could enjoy it.

1 cup butter (no substitutes), softened
2 cups sugar
4 eggs
1 teaspoon vanilla extract
4 cups all-purpose flour
4 teaspoons baking powder
1 teaspoon baking soda
2 cups (16 ounces) sour cream
2 cups (12 ounces) semisweet chocolate
   chips
GLAZE:
1/4 cup semisweet chocolate chips
2 tablespoons butter
1-1/4 cups confectioners' sugar
3 tablespoons milk
1/2 teaspoon vanilla extract

In a mixing bowl, cream butter and sugar. Add the eggs, one at a time, beating well after each addition. Beat in vanilla. Combine the flour, baking powder and baking soda; add to creamed mixture alternately with sour cream. Fold in chocolate chips. Pour into a greased and floured 10-in. fluted tube pan.

Bake at 350° for 60-65 minutes or until a toothpick inserted near the center comes out clean. Cool for 10 minutes before removing from pan to a wire rack to cool completely.

For glaze, in a saucepan over low heat, melt chocolate chips and butter. Remove from the heat; whisk in confectioners' sugar, milk and vanilla until smooth. Working quickly, drizzle over the cooled cake. **Yield:** 12-14 servings.

Sesame Pound Cake

Jane Finney, East Grand Forks, Minnesota

(Pictured above and on page 54)

This sesame seed-studded cake has a pleasant crunch. It's wonderful garnished with fresh fruit.

1 cup butter (no substitutes), softened
1 cup sugar
4 eggs
1/2 cup milk
1 teaspoon vanilla extract
1 teaspoon grated lemon peel
1/3 cup sesame seeds, toasted, *divided*
2 cups all-purpose flour
1 teaspoon baking powder
1/2 teaspoon salt

In a mixing bowl, cream butter and sugar. Beat in eggs, one at a time. Combine milk, vanilla and lemon peel; set aside. Reserve 1 tablespoon sesame seeds. Combine remaining sesame seeds with flour, baking powder and salt. Add dry ingredients to creamed mixture alternately with milk mixture; mix well. Pour into a greased and floured 9-in. x 5-in. x 3-in. loaf pan. Sprinkle with reserved sesame seeds.

Bake at 325° for 60-70 minutes or until a toothpick comes out clean. Cool in pan for 10 minutes; remove to a wire rack to cool completely. **Yield:** 8-10 servings.

Butter Basics

ALWAYS use butter or regular margarine (containing no less than 80% vegetable oil) when making cakes. Don't use light or whipped butter, diet spreads or tub margarine.

Chocolate Berry Pound Cake

Christi Ross, Guthrie, Texas

(Pictured above and on page 54)

This moist cake topped with raspberry whipped cream is from a dear friend's vast recipe collection. It tastes like something Grandma would make.

> 1 jar (10 ounces) seedless blackberry *or* black raspberry spreadable fruit, *divided*
> 2/3 cup butter *or* margarine, softened
> 1-1/2 cups sugar
> 2 eggs
> 1 teaspoon vanilla extract
> 2 cups all-purpose flour
> 3/4 cup baking cocoa
> 1-1/2 teaspoons baking soda
> 1 teaspoon salt
> 2 cups (16 ounces) sour cream
> Confectioners' sugar, optional
> RASPBERRY CREAM:
> 1 package (10 ounces) frozen sweetened raspberries, thawed
> 1 carton (8 ounces) frozen whipped topping, thawed
> Fresh raspberries and blackberries, optional

Place 3/4 cup of spreadable fruit in a microwave-safe bowl. Cover and microwave on high for 40-60 seconds or until melted; set aside. In a mixing bowl, cream butter and sugar. Add eggs and vanilla; mix well. Combine the flour, cocoa, baking soda and salt. Combine sour cream and melted fruit spread; add to creamed mixture alternately with dry ingredients. Pour into a greased and floured 10-in. fluted tube pan.

Bake at 350° for 50-55 minutes or until a toothpick inserted near the center comes out clean. Cool for 10 minutes before removing from pan to a wire rack. Place remaining spreadable fruit in a microwave-safe bowl. Cover and microwave on high for 20-30 seconds or until melted. Brush over warm cake. Cool. Dust with confectioners' sugar if desired.

For raspberry cream, puree raspberries in a blender or food processor; strain and discard seeds. Fold in the whipped topping. Serve with the cake. Garnish with fresh berries if desired. **Yield:** 10-12 servings.

Editor's Note: This recipe was tested in an 850-watt microwave.

Pumpkin Pound Cake

Virginia Loew, Leesburg, Florida

This cake is perfect for fall. As it bakes, the aroma fills the house with a spicy scent.

> 2-1/2 cups sugar
> 1 cup vegetable oil
> 3 eggs
> 3 cups all-purpose flour
> 2 teaspoons baking soda
> 1 teaspoon ground cinnamon
> 1 teaspoon ground nutmeg
> 1/2 teaspoon salt
> 1/4 teaspoon ground cloves
> 1 can (15 ounces) solid-pack pumpkin
> Confectioners' sugar

In a mixing bowl, blend sugar and oil. Add eggs, one at a time, beating well after each addition. Combine flour, baking soda, cinnamon, nutmeg, salt and cloves; add to egg mixture alternately with pumpkin. Transfer to a greased and floured 12-cup fluted tube pan.

Bake at 350° for 60-65 minutes or until a toothpick comes out clean. Cool for 10 minutes before removing from pan to a wire rack to cool completely. Dust with confectioners' sugar. **Yield:** 12-16 servings.

p. 67

p. 66

p. 67

p. 65

p. 64

Clockwise from top left: Rhubarb Upside-Down Cake, Spiced Pineapple Upside-Down Cake, Upside-Down Apple Gingerbread, Apricot Upside-Down Cake and Plum Upside-Down Cake.

Upside-Down Cakes

Apricot Upside-Down Cake

Ruth Ann Stelfox, Raymond, Alberta

(Pictured below and on page 62)

My Aunt Anne, who is a great cook, gave me a taste of this golden cake and I couldn't believe how delicious it was. Apricots give it an elegant twist.

> 2 cans (15 ounces *each*) apricot halves
> 1/4 cup butter *or* margarine
> 1/2 cup packed brown sugar
> 2 eggs, *separated*
> 2/3 cup sugar
> 2/3 cup cake flour
> 3/4 teaspoon baking powder
> 1/4 teaspoon salt

Drain apricots, reserving 3 tablespoons juice (discard remaining juice or save for another use); set aside. Place butter in a greased 9-in. square baking pan; place in a 350° oven for 3-4 minutes or until melted. Stir in the brown sugar. Arrange apricot halves, cut side up, in a single layer over sugar.

In a mixing bowl, beat egg yolks on high for 4 minutes or until thick and lemon-colored. Gradually beat in sugar. Stir in reserved apricot juice. Combine flour, baking powder and salt; gradually add to egg yolk mixture. In another mixing bowl, beat egg whites until stiff. Fold into yolk mixture. Carefully spread over apricots.

Bake at 350° for 35-40 minutes or until a toothpick inserted near the center of cake comes out clean. Cool for 10 minutes before inverting onto a serving plate. **Yield:** 9 servings.

Banana Upside-Down Cake

Ruth Andrewson, Leavenworth, Washington

For a fun and distinctive way to use bananas, I recommends this upside-down cake.

> 1/2 cup packed brown sugar
> 2 tablespoons lemon juice, *divided*

Spiced Apple Upside-Down Cake

Mavis Diment, Marcus, Iowa

(Pictured above)

I like unusual desserts like this one. Judging from the condition of my recipe card, this must be very good—a well-worn card shows I've made it countless times.

> 1 jar (14 ounces) spiced apple rings
> 6 tablespoons butter *or* margarine, softened, *divided*
> 1/2 cup packed brown sugar
> 1/4 cup sliced almonds, toasted
> 1 egg
> 1/2 cup milk
> 1 teaspoon vanilla extract
> 1 cup all-purpose flour
> 1/2 cup sugar
> 1-1/2 teaspoons baking powder
> Whipped cream, optional

Drain the apple rings, reserving 1 tablespoon syrup; set apple rings aside. Melt 2 tablespoons butter; add brown sugar and reserved syrup. Spread evenly in a greased 8-in. round baking pan; sprinkle with almonds. Top with apple rings; set aside.

In a mixing bowl, beat egg, milk, vanilla and remaining butter. Combine flour, sugar and baking powder; add to egg mixture and mix well. Spoon over apple rings.

Bake at 350° for 35-40 minutes or until a toothpick inserted near the center comes out clean. Let stand for 5 minutes. Run a knife around the edge of pan; invert cake onto a serving plate. Cool. Serve with whipped cream if desired. **Yield:** 6-8 servings.

1 tablespoon butter *or* margarine
1/2 cup pecan halves
2 medium firm bananas, sliced
CAKE:
1-1/2 cups all-purpose flour
1/2 cup sugar
1 teaspoon baking soda
1 teaspoon baking powder
1/4 teaspoon salt
1/4 cup cold butter *or* margarine
1 cup plain yogurt
2 eggs, beaten
2 teaspoons grated lemon peel
1 teaspoon vanilla extract
Whipped cream, optional

In a small saucepan, combine brown sugar, 1 tablespoon of lemon juice and butter; bring to a boil. Reduce heat to medium; cook without stirring until sugar is dissolved. Pour into a greased 9-in. springform pan. Arrange pecans on top with flat side up. Pour remaining lemon juice into a small bowl; add bananas and stir carefully. Drain. Arrange bananas in a circular pattern over the pecans; set aside.

In a large bowl, combine flour, sugar, baking soda, baking powder and salt. Cut in butter until mixture resembles coarse crumbs. Combine yogurt, eggs, lemon peel and vanilla; stir into the dry ingredients just until moistened. Spoon over bananas.

Bake at 375° for 35-40 minutes or until a toothpick comes out clean. Cool for 10 minutes. Run a knife around edge of pan; invert cake onto a serving plate. Serve with whipped cream if desired. **Yield:** 6-8 servings.

Plum Upside-Down Cake

Bobbie Talbott, Veneta, Oregon

(Pictured above and on page 62)

Years ago, a friend who was a fruit grower brought 20 pounds of lovely plums to my husband, Glenn, to thank him for some work Glenn had done on his car. Glenn invited him for dinner the next night, and I wanted to make a dessert using the plums.

1/3 cup butter *or* margarine
1/2 cup packed brown sugar
2 pounds fresh plums, pitted and halved
2 eggs
2/3 cup sugar
1 cup all-purpose flour
1 teaspoon baking powder
1/4 teaspoon salt
1/3 cup hot water
1/2 teaspoon lemon extract
Whipped cream, optional

Melt butter in a 10-in. cast-iron or ovenproof skillet. Sprinkle brown sugar over butter. Arrange plum halves, cut side down, in a single layer over sugar; set aside.

In a mixing bowl, beat eggs until thick and lemon-colored; gradually beat in sugar. Combine flour, baking powder and salt. Add to egg mixture; mix well. Blend water and lemon extract; beat into batter. Pour over plums.

Bake at 350° for 40-45 minutes or until a toothpick inserted near the center comes out clean. Immediately invert onto a serving plate. Serve warm with whipped cream if desired. **Yield:** 8-10 servings.

Upside-Down Apple Gingerbread

Florence Palmer, Marshall, Illinois

(Pictured below and on page 62)

Don't expect leftovers when you take this moist cake to a potluck. People love it because it's a little different and has a wonderful flavor. Try it for your next gathering.

        1/4 cup butter *or* margarine, melted
          2 large apples, peeled, cored and sliced
        1/3 cup packed brown sugar
    GINGERBREAD:
        1/2 cup butter *or* margarine, melted
        1/2 cup molasses
        1/2 cup sugar
        1/3 cup packed brown sugar
          1 egg
          2 cups all-purpose flour
          1 teaspoon baking soda
          1 teaspoon ground cinnamon
          1 teaspoon ground ginger
        1/2 teaspoon ground cloves
        1/2 teaspoon salt
        1/4 teaspoon ground nutmeg
        3/4 cup hot tea

Pour butter into a 9-in. square baking pan. Arrange apples over butter; sprinkle with brown sugar and set aside. For gingerbread, combine butter, molasses, sugars and egg in a mixing bowl; mix well. Combine dry ingredients; add to sugar mixture alternately with hot tea. Mix well; pour over apples.

Bake at 350° for 45-50 minutes or until a toothpick inserted near the center comes out clean. Cool for 3-5 minutes. Loosen sides and invert onto a serving plate. Serve warm. **Yield:** 9 servings.

Cranberry Upside-Down Cake

Ruth Marie Lyons, Boulder, Colorado

When I'm rushed for a dessert for a Christmas potluck, I grab the recipe for this old-fashioned cake. A cake mix gets special treatment from walnuts, pineapple and cranberries.

          1 can (20 ounces) pineapple tidbits
        1/2 cup butter *or* margarine, melted
          1 cup packed brown sugar
          1 cup fresh *or* frozen cranberries
        1/2 cup walnut halves
          1 package (18-1/4 ounces) yellow cake mix
          3 eggs
        1/4 cup vegetable oil

Drain pineapple, reserving juice. Add water to juice to measure 1-1/4 cups; set aside. Pour butter into a greased 13-in. x 9-in. x 2-in. baking dish. Sprinkle with

brown sugar, cranberries and walnuts. Top with pineapple. In a mixing bowl, combine dry cake mix, eggs, oil and reserved pineapple juice. Beat on medium speed for 2 minutes. Pour into prepared pan.

Bake at 350° for 25-35 minutes or until a toothpick inserted near the center comes out clean. Cool for 10 minutes before inverting onto a large serving platter. **Yield:** 12-16 servings.

Spiced Pineapple Upside-Down Cake

Jennifer Sergesketter, Newburgh, Indiana

(Pictured above and on page 62)

I often bake this beautiful cake in my large iron skillet and turn it out on a pizza pan.

1-1/3 cups butter *or* margarine, softened, *divided*
   1 cup packed brown sugar
   1 can (20 ounces) pineapple slices, drained
  10 to 12 maraschino cherries
  1/2 cup chopped pecans
1-1/2 cups sugar
   2 eggs
   1 teaspoon vanilla extract
   2 cups all-purpose flour
   2 teaspoons baking powder
  1/2 teaspoon baking soda
  1/2 teaspoon salt
  1/2 teaspoon ground cinnamon
  1/2 teaspoon ground nutmeg
   1 cup buttermilk

In a small saucepan, melt 2/3 cup of butter; stir in brown sugar. Spread in the bottom of an ungreased heavy 12-in. skillet or a 13-in. x 9-in. x 2-in. baking pan. Arrange pineapple in a single layer over sugar mixture; place a cherry in the center of each slice. Sprinkle with pecans and set aside.

In a mixing bowl, cream sugar and remaining butter. Beat in eggs and vanilla. Combine the dry ingredients; add alternately to batter with buttermilk, mixing well after each addition. Carefully pour over the pineapple.

Bake at 350° for 40 minutes for skillet (50-60 minutes

for baking pan) or until a toothpick inserted near the center comes out clean. Immediately invert onto a serving platter. **Yield:** 12 servings.

Rhubarb Upside-Down Cake

Helen Breman, Mattydale, New York

(Pictured below and on page 62)

I've baked this cake every spring for many years, and my family loves it! It disappears quickly.

TOPPING:
   3 cups fresh rhubarb, cut into 1/2-inch slices
   1 cup sugar
   2 tablespoons all-purpose flour
  1/4 teaspoon ground nutmeg
  1/4 cup butter *or* margarine, melted
BATTER:
1-1/2 cups all-purpose flour
  3/4 cup sugar
   2 teaspoons baking powder
  1/4 teaspoon salt
  1/2 teaspoon ground nutmeg
  1/4 cup butter *or* margarine, melted
  2/3 cup milk
   1 egg
Sweetened whipped cream, optional

Sprinkle rhubarb in a greased 10-in. heavy ovenproof skillet. Combine sugar, flour and nutmeg; sprinkle over rhubarb. Drizzle with butter. For batter, combine flour, sugar, baking powder, salt and nutmeg in a mixing bowl. Add butter, milk and egg; beat until smooth. Spread over rhubarb mixture.

Bake at 350° for 35 minutes or until a toothpick inserted near the center comes out clean. Loosen edges immediately and invert onto serving dish. Serve warm, topped with whipped cream if desired. **Yield:** 8-10 servings.

p. 70

p. 74

p. 78

p. 78

p. 77

Clockwise from top left: Chocolate Chiffon Valentine Cake, Marble Chiffon Cake, Orange Chiffon Cake, Sponge Cake with Blueberry Topping and Mocha Angel Food Torte.

Angel Food, Chiffon & Sponge Cakes

Chocolate Chiffon Valentine Cake

Pat Eastman, Provo, Utah

(Pictured below and on page 68)

I first made this lovely lightly textured cake for my husband for Valentine's Day more than 25 years ago. It's perfect for any special occasion. As an alternative, I've decorated the top with chocolate kisses.

  1/2 cup baking cocoa
  1/2 cup hot water
1-1/4 cups sugar, *divided*
  3/4 cup all-purpose flour
  3/4 teaspoon baking soda
  1/2 teaspoon salt
    4 eggs, *separated*
  1/4 cup vegetable oil
    1 teaspoon vanilla extract
  1/4 teaspoon cream of tartar
FROSTING:
1-1/2 cups whipping cream
  1/4 cup confectioners' sugar
  15 small fresh strawberries, halved
Fresh mint, optional

In a small bowl, combine cocoa and water until smooth; cool. In a large mixing bowl, combine 1 cup sugar, flour, baking soda and salt. Add egg yolks, oil, vanilla and cocoa mixture; stir until smooth. In a small mixing bowl, beat egg whites until foamy. Add cream of tartar; beat for 1 minute. Gradually add the remaining sugar, beating until soft peaks form. Gradually fold into chocolate mixture.

Pour into two greased and floured 9-in. heart-shaped pans or two 9-in. round baking pans. Bake at 350° for 18-20 minutes or until top springs back when lightly touched. Cool for 10 minutes before removing from pans to wire racks to cool completely.

In a mixing bowl, beat cream and confectioners' sugar. Spread frosting between layers and over top and sides of cake. Spoon 1-1/2 cups of frosting into a pastry bag with a star tip. Pipe a decorative lattice design on cake top and sides. Garnish with strawberries and mint if desired. Store in the refrigerator. **Yield:** 12 servings.

Chocolate Angel Cake

Joyce Shiffler, Manitou Springs, Colorado

(Pictured at right)

When I married in 1944, I could barely boil water. My dear mother-in-law taught me her specialty—making the lightest of angel food cakes ever. This chocolate version is an easy, impressive treat.

1-1/2 cups confectioners' sugar
    1 cup cake flour
  1/4 cup baking cocoa

Chiffon Cake

Arlene Murphy, Beverly Hills, Florida

(Pictured below)

My light and spongy cake makes a fitting finale to any meal, especially when it's dressed up with a drizzle of chocolate sauce.

      6 eggs, *separated*
  1/2 teaspoon salt
1-1/2 cups sugar, *divided*
  1/2 cup warm water
1-1/2 cups all-purpose flour, *divided*
      1 teaspoon vanilla extract
  1/2 teaspoon cream of tartar
  1/2 cup chocolate ice cream topping

In a mixing bowl, beat egg yolks and salt for 2 minutes. Gradually beat in 1 cup sugar; beat 2 minutes longer. Gradually add water; beat about 2-1/2 minutes longer or until frothy. Beat in 3/4 cup flour. Beat in vanilla and remaining flour.

In another mixing bowl, beat egg whites until foamy. Add cream of tartar; beat until soft peaks form. Gradually beat in remaining sugar, 1 tablespoon at a time, on high until stiff peaks form. Fold into egg yolk mixture.

Pour into an ungreased 10-in. tube pan. Bake on lowest oven rack at 325° for 55-60 minutes or until top springs back when lightly touched and cracks feel dry. Immediately invert pan onto a wire rack; cool completely. Run a knife around edges and center tube to loosen; remove cake. Slice; drizzle with ice cream topping. **Yield:** 12 servings.

1-1/2 cups egg whites (about 10 eggs)
1-1/2 teaspoons cream of tartar
  1/2 teaspoon salt
    1 cup sugar
FROSTING:
1-1/2 cups whipping cream
  1/2 cup sugar
  1/4 cup baking cocoa
  1/2 teaspoon salt
  1/2 teaspoon vanilla extract
Chocolate leaves, optional

Sift together confectioners' sugar, flour and cocoa three times; set aside. In a mixing bowl, beat egg whites, cream of tartar and salt until soft peaks form. Add sugar, 2 tablespoons at a time, beating until stiff peaks form. Gradually fold in cocoa mixture, a fourth at a time.

Spoon into an ungreased 10-in. tube pan. Carefully run a metal spatula or knife through batter to remove air pockets. Bake on lowest oven rack at 375° for 35-40 minutes or until the top springs back when lightly touched and cracks feel dry. Immediately invert pan; cool completely. Run a knife around edges and center tube to loosen; remove cake.

In a mixing bowl, combine the first five frosting ingredients; cover and chill for 1 hour. Beat until stiff peaks form. Spread over top and sides of cake. Store in the refrigerator. Garnish with chocolate leaves if desired. **Yield:** 12-16 servings.

Cooling Foam Cakes

ANGEL FOOD, chiffon and sponge cakes are cooled by inverting the pan, which keeps the cakes from falling.

Banana Chiffon Cake

Nancy Horsburgh, Everett, Ontario

(Pictured above)

Simple yet delicious desserts were my Aunt Allie's specialty. This cake was one of her best.

2-1/4 cups cake flour
1-1/2 cups sugar
    1 tablespoon baking powder
    1 teaspoon salt
    1 cup mashed ripe bananas (about 2 medium)
    1/3 cup vegetable oil
    1/3 cup water
    5 eggs, *separated*
    1 teaspoon vanilla extract
Chocolate frosting *or* **frosting of your choice**

In a large bowl, combine flour, sugar, baking powder and salt. Make a well in the center; add bananas, oil, water, egg yolks and vanilla. Beat until smooth. In a small mixing bowl, beat egg whites until stiff peaks form. Fold into batter. Pour into an ungreased 10-in. tube pan.

Bake on lowest oven rack at 325° for 60-65 minutes or until cake springs back when lightly touched. Immediately invert pan; cool completely. Run a knife around edges and center tube to loosen; remove cake. Frost top and sides. **Yield:** 12 servings.

Midsummer Sponge Cake

Robin Fuhrman, Fond du Lac, Wisconsin

(Pictured at right)

People like everything about this dessert—the tender cake layers, fluffy cream filling and fresh fruit topping.

    4 eggs
1-1/4 cups sugar
1-1/4 cups all-purpose flour

    2 teaspoons baking powder
    1/2 cup water
 1-1/2 cups cold milk
    1/2 teaspoon vanilla extract
    1 package (3.4 ounces) instant vanilla pudding mix
    2 cups whipped topping
    3 tablespoons lemon gelatin powder
    1/2 cup boiling water
Assorted fresh fruit

In a mixing bowl, beat eggs until light and fluffy. Gradually beat in sugar until light and lemon-colored. Combine flour and baking powder; add to egg mixture alternately with water, beating just until smooth. Pour into a greased and floured 10-in. springform pan. Bake at 375° for 20-25 minutes or until cake springs back when lightly touched. Cool on a wire rack for 1 hour.

Carefully run a knife around edge of pan; remove sides. Invert onto a wire rack. Remove bottom of pan; invert cake so top is up. Using a sharp knife, split cake in half horizontally; set aside.

For filling, in a mixing bowl, beat milk, vanilla and pudding mix for 2 minutes or until thickened; chill for 10 minutes. Fold in whipped topping. For glaze, dissolve gelatin in boiling water. Add enough cold water to measure 1 cup. Chill for 15 minutes or until slightly thickened. To assemble, place bottom cake layer on a cake plate. Spread filling over cake; top with second cake layer and fruit. Drizzle with glaze. Store in the refrigerator. **Yield:** 10-12 servings.

Cinnamon-Apple Angel Food Cake

Marlys Benning, Wellsburg, Iowa

This heavenly dessert is as light as a feather and melts in your mouth. The cinnamon-apple glaze is delightful.

1-1/2 cups egg whites (about 12 eggs)
1-1/2 teaspoons cream of tartar
    1/4 teaspoon salt
    1 cup sugar
    1 teaspoon vanilla extract
    1/2 teaspoon almond extract
1-1/2 cups confectioners' sugar

1 cup cake flour
GLAZE:
   1/3 cup butter *or* margarine
   2 cups confectioners' sugar
   1/2 teaspoon ground cinnamon
   3 to 4 tablespoons apple juice *or* cider

In a mixing bowl, beat egg whites, cream of tartar and salt on medium speed until soft peaks form. Add sugar, 2 tablespoons at a time, beating well after each addition; beat until smooth and glossy and stiff peaks form. Add extracts on low speed. Combine confectioners' sugar and flour; gently fold into egg mixture.

Pour into an ungreased 10-in. tube pan. Bake on lowest oven rack at 375° for 35-40 minutes or until top springs back when lightly touched and cracks feel dry. Immediately invert cake in pan to cool completely. Run a knife around edges and center tube to loosen; remove cake.

For glaze, melt butter in a saucepan. Stir in the confectioners' sugar and cinnamon. Add apple juice slowly until glaze is thin enough to drizzle. Drizzle over cake. **Yield:** 12-16 servings.

Poppy Seed Chiffon Cake

Irene Hirsch, Tustin, California

(Pictured above)

This cake is quite easy to make and everyone who tries it tells me how good it tastes. The lemon frosting really accents the flavor of the cake.

2-1/2 cups all-purpose flour
   1 cup sugar
   1 tablespoon baking powder
   1/2 teaspoon salt
   3/4 cup water
   1/2 cup vegetable oil
   5 egg yolks
   1 teaspoon lemon extract
   1 teaspoon grated lemon peel
   1 can (12-1/2 ounces) poppy seed filling
   7 egg whites
   1/2 teaspoon cream of tartar
LEMON BUTTER FROSTING:
   6 tablespoons butter *or* margarine, softened
   4 cups confectioners' sugar
   3 to 5 tablespoons milk
   1 tablespoon lemon juice
   1 teaspoon lemon extract

In a mixing bowl, combine flour, sugar, baking powder and salt. Add water, oil, egg yolks, lemon extract, lemon peel and filling; beat until smooth. In another bowl, beat egg whites and cream of tartar until stiff peaks form. Fold into batter; pour into an ungreased 10-in. tube pan.

Bake on lowest oven rack at 350° for 55-60 minutes or until cake springs back when lightly touched. Immediately invert pan; cool completely. Run a knife around edges and center tube to loosen; remove cake.

For frosting, cream the butter and sugar in a mixing bowl. Add the milk, lemon juice and extract; beat until smooth. Frost top and sides of cake. **Yield:** 12-16 servings.

Marble Chiffon Cake

Sharon Evans, Rockwell, Iowa

(Pictured above and on page 68)

This high cake won a blue ribbon for "best chiffon cake" at our county fair one year.

  1/3 cup baking cocoa
  1/4 cup boiling water
1-1/2 cups plus 3 tablespoons sugar, *divided*
  1/2 cup plus 2 tablespoons vegetable oil, *divided*
2-1/4 cups all-purpose flour
  1 tablespoon baking powder
  1 teaspoon salt
  7 eggs, *separated*
  3/4 cup water
  1/2 teaspoon cream of tartar
  2 teaspoons grated orange peel
ORANGE GLAZE:
  2 cups confectioners' sugar
  1/3 cup butter *or* margarine, melted
  3 to 4 tablespoons orange juice
  1/2 teaspoon grated orange peel

In a bowl, combine cocoa, boiling water, 3 tablespoons sugar and 2 tablespoons oil; whisk until smooth. Cool. In a mixing bowl, combine flour, baking powder, salt and remaining sugar. Whisk egg yolks, water and remaining oil; add to dry ingredients. Beat until well blended. Beat egg whites and cream of tartar until soft peaks form; fold into batter.

Remove 2 cups of batter; stir into cocoa mixture. To the remaining batter, add orange peel. Alternately spoon the batters into an ungreased 10-in. tube pan. Swirl with a knife. Bake at 325° for 70-75 minutes or until top springs back when lightly touched. Invert cake pan on a wire rack; cool. For the glaze, combine sugar, butter and enough or-

ange juice to reach desired consistency. Add orange peel; spoon over cake. **Yield:** 12-14 servings.

Sunny Sponge Cake

Candy Snyder, Salem, Oregon

(Pictured below)

This golden cake has a light texture and mild orange flavor that makes it a pleasant ending to most any meal. The spongy interior is moist, tender and flecked with bits of orange peel.

  3 egg yolks
  1 cup sugar, *divided*
  2 teaspoons hot water
  1/2 cup orange juice, warmed
1-1/4 teaspoons vanilla extract
  3/4 teaspoon grated orange peel
  1/4 teaspoon grated lemon peel
1-1/2 cups all-purpose flour
1-1/4 teaspoons baking powder
  1/4 teaspoon salt
  6 egg whites
Whipped topping

In a mixing bowl, beat egg yolks until slightly thickened. Gradually add 3/4 cup sugar and hot water, beating until thick and lemon-colored. Blend in the orange juice, vanilla and orange and lemon peels. Sift together the flour, baking powder and salt; add to egg yolk mixture.

In another mixing bowl, beat the egg whites until soft peaks form. Add the remaining sugar, 1 tablespoon at a time, beating until stiff peaks form. Fold a fourth of the egg whites into the batter; fold in remaining whites.

Spoon into an ungreased 10-in. tube pan. Bake on lowest oven rack at 350° for 20-25 minutes or until cake springs back when lightly touched. Immediately invert pan; cool completely. Cut into slices; serve with whipped topping. **Yield:** 12 servings.

Lime Angel Food Cake

Nancy Foust, Stoneboro, Pennsylvania

It's fun to start with a purchased angel food cake and turn out a special dessert. A lovely lime cream frosting is the key to this dressy, flavorful creation.

      2 eggs
      2 egg yolks
  1/2 cup plus 3 tablespoons sugar, *divided*
      6 tablespoons lime juice
      2 teaspoons grated lime peel
  1/2 cup cold butter *or* margarine, cubed
      1 cup whipping cream
  1/2 teaspoon vanilla extract
      1 prepared angel food cake (10 inches)
      1 cup flaked coconut, toasted

In the top of a double boiler, beat eggs and yolks. Stir in 1/2 cup of sugar, lime juice and peel. Cook over simmering water while gradually whisking in butter. Cook and stir until mixture is thickened and reaches 160°. Strain; refrigerate until completely cool. In a mixing bowl, beat cream and vanilla until stiff peaks form; gradually beat in remaining sugar. Gently fold into lime mixture.

Split cake horizontally into three layers. Place bottom layer on a serving plate. Spread with 2/3 cup lime mixture. Repeat. Place top layer on cake. Frost top and sides with remaining lime mixture. Sprinkle with coconut. Refrigerate for at least 30 minutes before slicing. Store in the refrigerator. **Yield:** 12 servings.

Marbled Peppermint Angel Cake

Kathy Kittell, Lenexa, Kansas

Although it doesn't puff up as much as other angel food cakes during baking, the minty flavor and festive red swirls raise this version above ordinary desserts!

1-1/2 cups egg whites (about 12)
1-1/2 teaspoons cream of tartar
1-1/2 teaspoons vanilla extract
      1 teaspoon peppermint extract
  1/4 teaspoon salt
1-1/2 cups sugar, *divided*
  3/4 cup all-purpose flour
      6 drops red food coloring, optional
GLAZE:
      2 cups confectioners' sugar
  1/4 cup milk
  1/4 teaspoon peppermint extract
      6 drops red food coloring, optional
  1/4 cup crushed peppermint candies

In a mixing bowl, beat egg whites, cream of tartar, extracts and salt on high speed. Gradually add 3/4 cup of sugar, beating until stiff peaks form and sugar is dissolved. Combine flour and remaining sugar; gradually fold into the batter, 1/4 cup at a time. Divide batter in half; tint half with red food coloring. Alternately spoon plain and pink batters into an ungreased 10-in. tube pan.

Cut through batter with a knife to remove air pockets.

Bake on the lowest oven rack at 350° for 30-40 minutes or until cake springs back when lightly touched. Immediately invert pan; cool completely. Run a knife around edges and center tube to loosen; remove cake. For glaze, combine confectioners' sugar, milk, extract and food coloring if desired. Drizzle over cake. Sprinkle with candies. **Yield:** 12-16 servings.

Angel Berry Tunnel Cake

Ruth Marie Lyons, Boulder, Colorado

(Pictured above)

This tasty cake is a light favorite for summer. To save time, rely on a purchased angel food cake and frozen whipped topping.

      1 prepared angel food cake (10 inches)
1-1/2 cups fresh *or* frozen raspberries, thawed
        and drained
1-1/2 cups fresh *or* frozen blueberries
      8 cups whipped topping
Additional berries

With a serrated knife, slice off the top 1/2 in. of the cake; set aside. Cut a tunnel about 2 in. deep in the cake, leaving a 3/4-in. shell. Remove cake from tunnel; cut into 1-in. cubes. Combine cake cubes, berries and half of the whipped topping; spoon into tunnel. Replace cake top. Frost with remaining whipped topping. Garnish with berries. Store in the refrigerator. **Yield:** 12 servings.

Angel Food Cake with Caramel Sauce

Carolyn Troyer, Sugarcreek, Ohio

(Pictured below)

I enjoy making desserts, and it's especially satisfying when my goodies are devoured quickly. This one always qualifies for that distinction.

> 1 package (3 ounces) cream cheese, softened
> 1/4 cup confectioners' sugar
> 1 carton (8 ounces) frozen whipped topping, thawed
> 1 prepared angel food cake (10 inches)
> **CARAMEL SAUCE:**
> 1 cup half-and-half cream, *divided*
> 3/4 cup sugar
> 1/2 cup light corn syrup
> 1/4 cup butter (no substitutes)
> Pinch salt
> 1/2 teaspoon vanilla extract

In a mixing bowl, beat cream cheese and confectioners' sugar until smooth. Fold in whipped topping; set aside. Cut cake horizontally into two layers. Place the bottom layer on a serving plate; spread with cream cheese mixture. Replace top; refrigerate.

In a saucepan, combine 3/4 cup of cream, sugar, corn syrup, butter and salt. Cook and stir until mixture reaches soft-ball stage (234°). Slowly add remaining cream. Cook and stir until mixture returns to soft-ball stage (234°). Remove from the heat; stir in vanilla. Cool. Drizzle over cake. Store in the refrigerator. **Yield:** 12 servings.

Layered Toffee Cake

Pat Squire, Alexandria, Virginia

(Pictured above)

This is a quick and yummy way to dress up a purchased angel food cake.

> 2 cups whipping cream
> 1/2 cup caramel *or* butterscotch ice cream topping
> 1/2 teaspoon vanilla extract
> 1 prepared angel food cake (16 ounces)
> 9 Heath candy bars (1.4 ounces *each*), chopped

In a mixing bowl, beat cream just until it begins to thicken. Gradually add the ice cream topping and vanilla, beating until soft peaks form. Cut cake horizontally into three layers. Place the bottom layer on a serving plate; spread with 1 cup cream mixture and sprinkle with 1/2 cup candy bar. Repeat. Place top layer on cake; frost top and sides with remaining cream mixture and sprinkle with the remaining candy bar. Store in the refrigerator. **Yield:** 12-14 servings.

Cutting Cakes

CUT foam cakes with a serrated knife or an electric knife with a back-and-forth or sawing motion.

Chocolate Chiffon Cake

Dorothy Haag, Mt. Horeb, Wisconsin

There were 11 of us to cook for when I was young. This was a favorite dessert that my mother made often over the years. If there were cracked eggs from the laying hens she kept, it was always a good way to use them up!

2/3 cup baking cocoa
3/4 cup hot water
1-1/2 cups cake flour
1-3/4 cups sugar
1 teaspoon baking soda
1 teaspoon salt
1/2 cup vegetable oil
7 eggs, *separated*
1 teaspoon vanilla extract
1/2 teaspoon cream of tartar
Confectioners' sugar

In a small bowl, stir cocoa and water until smooth; cool. In a large bowl, combine flour, sugar, baking soda and salt. Add oil, egg yolks, vanilla and cocoa mixture; stir until smooth.

In a mixing bowl, beat the egg whites until foamy. Add cream of tartar; beat until stiff peaks form. Gradually fold in egg yolk mixture.

Pour into an ungreased 10-in. tube pan. Bake on lowest oven rack at 325° for 60-65 minutes or until the top springs back when lightly touched and cracks feel dry. Immediately invert pan; cool completely. Run a knife around edges and center tube to loosen; remove cake. Dust with confectioners' sugar. **Yield:** 12-16 servings.

Mocha Angel Food Torte

Hillary Brunn, Santa Rosa, California

(Pictured below and on page 68)

Chocolate, toffee and a hint of coffee make this pretty torte a popular request at my house. I use a few instant ingredients I usually have on hand to give prepared angel food cake homespun flair.

1-1/3 cups cold milk
1 package (3.9 ounces) instant chocolate pudding mix
1 tablespoon instant coffee granules
1 cup whipping cream, whipped, *divided*
1 prepared angel food cake (10 inches)
2 Heath candy bars (1.4 ounces *each*), crushed

In a mixing bowl, combine milk, pudding mix and coffee; beat on low speed for 2 minutes or until thickened. Fold in half of the whipped cream.

Cut cake in half horizontally; place the bottom layer on a serving plate. Spread with half of the pudding mixture. Top with remaining cake.

Fold remaining whipped cream into remaining pudding mixture; spread over top and sides of cake. Sprinkle with crushed candy bars. Chill for 2 hours before serving. Store in the refrigerator. **Yield:** 10-12 servings.

Orange Chiffon Cake

Marjorie Ebert, South Dayton, New York

(Pictured above and on page 68)

It wasn't until a few years ago that I started entering our county fair. Since then, this cake has been awarded several blue ribbons.

- **2 cups all-purpose flour**
- **1-1/2 cups sugar**
- **4 teaspoons baking powder**
- **1 teaspoon salt**
- **6 eggs, *separated***
- **3/4 cup fresh orange juice**
- **1/2 cup vegetable oil**
- **2 tablespoons grated orange peel**
- **1/2 teaspoon cream of tartar**
- **ORANGE GLAZE:**
- **1/2 cup butter *or* margarine**
- **2 cups confectioners' sugar**
- **2 to 4 tablespoons fresh orange juice**
- **1/2 teaspoon grated orange peel**

In a large mixing bowl, combine the first four ingredients. Add egg yolks, orange juice, oil and peel; beat until smooth, about 5 minutes. In another mixing bowl, beat egg whites and cream of tartar until stiff but not dry. Fold into orange mixture. Spoon into an ungreased 10-in. tube pan.

Bake on the lowest oven rack at 350° for 45-50 min-

utes or until top springs back when lightly touched. Immediately invert pan to cool. Run a knife around edges and center tube to loosen; remove cake.

For glaze, melt butter in a small saucepan; add remaining ingredients. Stir until smooth. Pour over top of cake, allowing it to drizzle down sides. **Yield:** 16 servings.

Sponge Cake with Blueberry Topping

Frances Cooley, Coos Bay, Oregon

(Pictured at right and on page 68)

This recipe puts the blueberries grown in our area to good use. It's a great summertime dessert.

- **6 eggs, *separated***
- **1-1/2 cups sugar**
- **3/4 cup orange juice**
- **1-1/2 cups all-purpose flour**
- **1-1/2 teaspoons baking powder**
- **1/4 teaspoon cream of tartar**
- **BLUEBERRY TOPPING:**
- **1/2 cup sugar**
- **2 teaspoons cornstarch**
- **1 tablespoon grated orange peel**
- **1/2 cup orange juice**
- **2 cups fresh *or* frozen blueberries**

SOUR CREAM TOPPING:
    2 cups (16 ounces) sour cream
    1 tablespoon confectioners' sugar
    1 teaspoon vanilla extract
Shredded orange peel, optional

In a large mixing bowl, beat egg yolks for 4-5 minutes or until thickened and light yellow. Gradually add sugar, beating for 1-2 minutes or until sugar is dissolved. Add orange juice; beat for 2-3 minutes or until mixture slightly thickens. Combine flour and baking powder; gradually add to yolk mixture and mix well.

In a small mixing bowl, beat egg whites and cream of tartar until stiff peaks form. Fold into egg yolk mixture until well blended. Pour into an ungreased 10-in. tube pan. Bake on the lowest oven rack at 325° for 50-55 minutes or until cake springs back when lightly touched. Immediately invert pan to cool completely.

For blueberry topping, combine sugar, cornstarch and orange peel in a saucepan. Stir in orange juice until smooth. Bring to a boil; cook and stir for 2 minutes or until thickened. Remove from the heat. Stir in the blueberries.

In a bowl, combine the sour cream, confectioners' sugar and vanilla. Remove cooled cake from pan; cut into slices. Serve with warm blueberry topping and the sour cream topping. Garnish with orange peel if desired. **Yield:** 12-16 servings.

Strawberry Sunshine Cake

Rosemary Binette, Les Cedres, Quebec

(Pictured above right)

With fluffy whipped topping frosting and a fresh strawberry filling and garnish, this impressive three-layer sponge cake is a scrumptious dessert. For best results, be sure to slice it with a serrated knife.

    1 cup egg whites (about 8)
    1/2 teaspoon cream of tartar
    1/2 teaspoon salt
  1-1/2 cups sugar, *divided*
    5 egg yolks
    2 tablespoons water
    1/2 teaspoon *each* almond, lemon and vanilla
        extracts
    1 cup all-purpose flour
FILLING:
    1 package (3 ounces) strawberry gelatin
    1 cup boiling water
    1/2 cup ice water
    1 pint fresh strawberries, sliced
    1 carton (8 ounces) frozen whipped topping,
        thawed, *divided*
Additional strawberries for garnish

In a large mixing bowl, beat egg whites, cream of tartar and salt until soft peaks form. Gradually add 1 cup sugar, a tablespoon at a time, beating until stiff peaks form; set aside.

In another bowl, beat egg yolks until slightly thickened, about 5 minutes. Gradually add remaining sugar, beating until thick and lemon-colored. Blend in water and extracts. Sift flour over batter; beat until smooth. Fold in egg whites just until blended.

Spoon into an ungreased 10-in. tube pan. Cut through batter with a knife to remove air pockets; smooth the top. Bake on the lowest oven rack at 325° for 50-55 minutes or until cake springs back when lightly touched. Immediately invert pan; cool completely.

In a bowl, dissolve gelatin in boiling water. Add ice water and stir. Place bowl in ice water for about 5 minutes or until slightly thickened. Fold in strawberries and 1/2 cup whipped topping.

Run a knife around edges and center tube to loosen; remove cake. Split horizontally into three layers; place bottom layer on a serving plate. Spread with half of the gelatin mixture. Repeat. Top with remaining cake layer. Frost top and sides with remaining whipped topping. Garnish with strawberries. Store in the refrigerator. **Yield:** 12-16 servings.

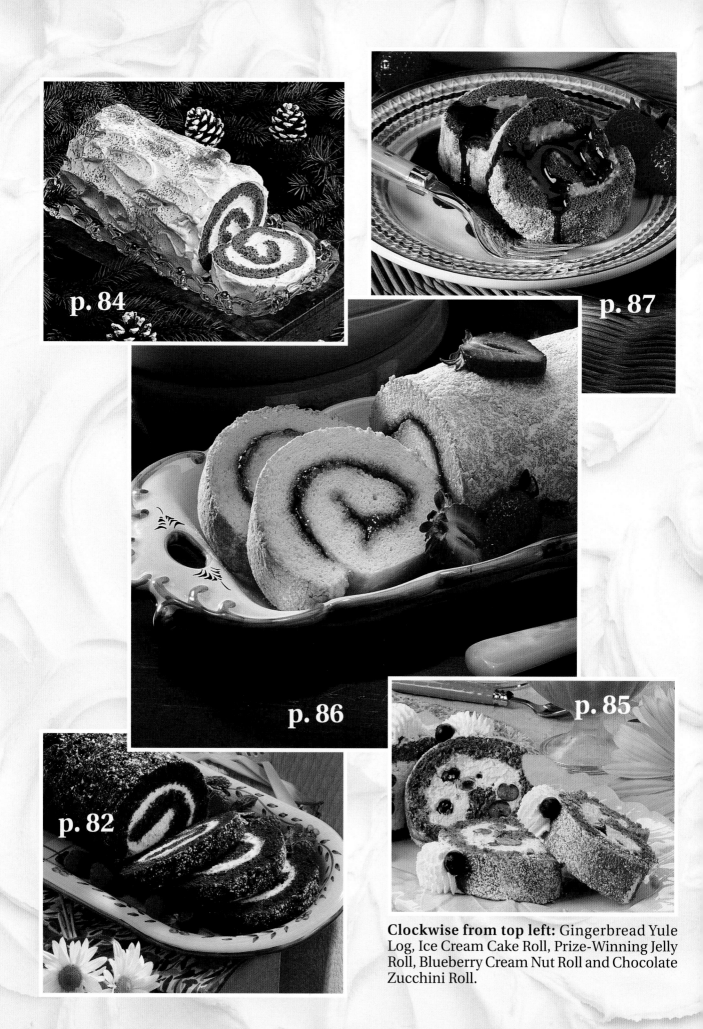

p. 84

p. 87

p. 86

p. 85

p. 82

Clockwise from top left: Gingerbread Yule Log, Ice Cream Cake Roll, Prize-Winning Jelly Roll, Blueberry Cream Nut Roll and Chocolate Zucchini Roll.

Cake Rolls

Raspberry-Almond Jelly Roll

Gloria Warczak, Cedarburg, Wisconsin

(Pictured below)

I've been making this sensational cake for many years for all kinds of parties. With a whipped cream, almond and raspberry filling, the lovely swirled slices taste as good as they look.

        3 eggs
        1 cup sugar
    1/3 cup water
    1-1/2 teaspoons almond extract, *divided*
    1-1/2 teaspoons vanilla extract, *divided*
    3/4 cup cake flour
        1 teaspoon baking powder
    1/4 teaspoon salt
        2 cups whipping cream
    3/4 cup confectioners' sugar
    1-1/4 cups blanched slivered almonds, toasted,
            divided
    2/3 cup seedless raspberry jam
Fresh raspberries and mint, optional

In a mixing bowl, beat eggs until light and fluffy. Gradually beat in sugar. Beat in water, 1 teaspoon almond extract and 1/2 teaspoon vanilla. Combine flour, baking powder and salt; beat into egg mixture until smooth. Line a greased 15-in. x 10-in. x 1-in. baking pan with greased waxed paper. Spread batter evenly in pan.

Bake at 375° for 12-15 minutes or until the cake springs back when lightly touched. Cool in pan on a wire rack for 15 minutes. Turn onto a kitchen towel dusted with confectioners' sugar. Gently peel off waxed paper. Roll up cake in the towel, jelly-roll style, starting with a short side. Cool for 30 minutes.

Meanwhile, beat cream, confectioners' sugar and remaining extracts until soft peaks form. Place half of the whipped cream in another bowl and refrigerate. Chop 1 cup almonds; fold into remaining cream. Unroll cake; spread with jam to within 1/2 in. of edges. Spread with almond mixture. Reroll. Place, seam side down, on a serving plate. Frost with chilled whipped cream. Store in the refrigerator. Garnish with remaining almonds and raspberries and mint if desired. **Yield:** 10 servings.

Chocolate Zucchini Roll

Victoria Zmarzley-Hahn, Northampton, Pennsylvania

(Pictured above and on page 80)

I created this cake roll to use my garden zucchini. The combination of chocolate and zucchini is fantastic!

        3 eggs
        1 teaspoon vanilla extract
        1 cup all-purpose flour
    3/4 cup sugar
    1/2 cup baking cocoa
        1 teaspoon baking soda
        1 teaspoon ground cinnamon
    1/4 teaspoon salt
        1 cup shredded peeled zucchini
FILLING:
        1 package (8 ounces) cream cheese, softened
    1/4 cup butter *or* margarine, softened
        2 teaspoons vanilla extract
        1 cup confectioners' sugar
Additional confectioners' sugar

In a mixing bowl, beat eggs and vanilla. Combine flour, sugar, cocoa, baking soda, cinnamon and salt; add to egg mixture and mix well (batter will be thick). Stir in zucchini. Spread into a greased and waxed paper-lined 15-in. x 10-in. x 1-in. baking pan.

Bake at 350° for 10-15 minutes or until cake springs back when lightly touched. Turn onto a kitchen towel dusted with confectioners' sugar. Peel off waxed paper and roll up, jelly-roll style, starting with a short side. Cool on a wire rack.

In a mixing bowl, beat cream cheese, butter and vanilla until fluffy. Beat in confectioners' sugar. Unroll cake; spread filling to within 1 in. of edges. Roll up again; dust with confectioners' sugar. Refrigerate until serving. **Yield:** 10 servings.

Strawberry Nut Roll

Judy Hayes, Peosta, Iowa

(Pictured above)

I did a lot of baking growing up. Desserts like this refreshing rolled shortcake are my favorite.

6 eggs, *separated*
3/4 cup sugar, *divided*
1 cup ground walnuts, toasted
1/4 cup dry bread crumbs
1/4 cup all-purpose flour
1/8 teaspoon salt
Confectioners' sugar
FILLING:
1 pint fresh strawberries
1 cup whipping cream
2 tablespoons sugar
1 teaspoon vanilla extract
Confectioners' sugar

In a mixing bowl, beat egg whites until soft peaks form. Gradually add 1/4 cup sugar, beating until stiff peaks form. Set aside. In another mixing bowl, beat egg yolks and remaining sugar until thick and lemon-colored. Combine walnuts, bread crumbs, flour and salt; add to yolk mixture. Mix well. Fold in egg white mixture. Line a greased 15-in. x 10-in. x 1-in. baking pan with waxed paper; grease the paper. Spread batter evenly in pan.

Bake at 375° for 15 minutes or until cake springs back when lightly touched. Cool for 5 minutes. Invert cake onto a kitchen towel dusted with confectioners' sugar. Gently peel off waxed paper. Roll up cake in towel, jelly-roll style, starting with a short side. Cool on a wire rack.

Slice six large strawberries in half; set aside for garnish. Thinly slice remaining berries; set aside. In a mixing bowl, beat cream until soft peaks form. Gradually add sugar and vanilla, beating until stiff peaks form. Unroll cake; spread with filling to within 1/2 in. of edges. Top with sliced berries. Roll up again. Place, seam side down, on serving platter. Chill until serving. Dust with confectioners' sugar. Garnish with reserved strawberries. Refrigerate leftovers. **Yield:** 12 servings.

Lemon Cake Roll

Dorothy Earl, Lancaster, South Carolina

This recipe dates back quite a few years. My mother made it for me when I was a child.

3 eggs
1 cup sugar
3 tablespoons cold water
1 cup all-purpose flour
1 teaspoon baking powder
1/4 teaspoon salt
FILLING:
1 cup sugar
3 tablespoons all-purpose flour
1 egg, lightly beaten
3/4 cup water
1/4 cup lemon juice

In a mixing bowl, beat eggs and sugar until thick and smooth. Add water. Combine flour, baking powder and salt; stir into egg mixture just until moistened. Line a greased 15-in. x 10-in. x 1-in. baking pan with waxed paper; grease the paper. Spread batter evenly in pan.

Bake at 375° for 12-14 minutes or until cake springs back when lightly touched. Cool for 5 minutes. Invert cake onto a kitchen towel dusted with confectioners' sugar. Gently peel off the waxed paper. Beginning with short side, roll up cake, jelly-roll style. Cool on a wire rack.

For filling, in a saucepan, combine sugar, flour, egg, water and lemon juice. Cook and stir over medium heat until mixture comes to a boil. Cook and stir 1 minute longer until thickened. Remove from the heat; cool to room temperature. Unroll cake; spread cooled filling to within 1 in. of edges. Roll up again. Cover and chill for 1-2 hours before serving. Refrigerate leftovers. **Yield:** 10-12 servings.

Rhubarb Jelly-Roll Cake

Donna Stratton, Carson City, Nevada

(Pictured below)

This jelly-roll recipe came from my mom's cookbook, circa 1940. It's continued to be a family classic and is popular at church potlucks. Soon, I'll be introducing this rhubarb cake to kids in my 4-H cooking class.

        6 cups chopped fresh *or* frozen rhubarb,
            thawed
    2-3/4 cups sugar, *divided*
        2 teaspoons ground cinnamon
        1/4 teaspoon ground allspice
        1/8 teaspoon ground cloves
        4 eggs
        1 teaspoon lemon extract
        3/4 cup all-purpose flour
        1 teaspoon baking powder
    1/2 teaspoon salt
    Confectioners' sugar

In a saucepan, combine the rhubarb, 2 cups sugar, cinnamon, allspice and cloves. Bring to a boil. Reduce heat; cook, uncovered, over medium heat until thickened. Cool completely.

In a mixing bowl, beat eggs on high speed until thick and lemon-colored. Gradually add remaining sugar, beating until thick and light-colored. Beat in extract. Combine the flour, baking powder and salt; gradually add to egg mixture.

Grease a 15-in. x 10-in. x 1-in. baking pan and line with waxed paper; grease and flour the paper. Spread batter into pan. Bake at 375° for 15 minutes or until cake springs back when lightly touched. Cool for 5 minutes. Turn onto a kitchen towel dusted with confectioners' sugar. Peel off waxed paper. Roll up cake in towel jelly-roll style, starting with a short side. Cool.

Carefully unroll cake. Spread filling over cake to within 1 in. of edges. Roll up again. Store in the refrigerator. Dust with confectioners' sugar just before serving. **Yield:** 10-12 servings.

Gingerbread Yule Log

Bernadette Colvin, Houston, Texas

(Pictured above and on page 80)

Whenever our family gets together for the holidays, this is what I'm asked to bring.

        3 eggs, *separated*
    1/2 cup molasses
        1 tablespoon butter *or* margarine, melted
    1/4 cup sugar
        1 cup all-purpose flour
    3/4 teaspoon *each* baking powder and
            baking soda
    1/2 teaspoon *each* ground cinnamon, ginger
            and cloves
    1/8 teaspoon salt
    SPICED CREAM FILLING:
    1-1/2 cups whipping cream
    1/3 cup confectioners' sugar
        1 teaspoon ground cinnamon
        1 teaspoon vanilla extract
    1/4 teaspoon ground cloves
    Additional ground cinnamon, optional

In a mixing bowl, beat yolks on high until thickened, about 3 minutes. Beat in molasses and butter. In another bowl, beat whites until foamy; gradually add sugar, beating until soft peaks form. Fold into yolk mixture. Combine dry ingredients; gently fold into egg mixture until well mixed.

Line a greased 15-in. x 10-in. x 1-in. baking pan with waxed paper; grease and flour paper. Spread batter into pan. Bake at 375° for 9-12 minutes or until cake springs back when lightly touched. Turn onto a kitchen towel dusted with confectioners' sugar. Peel off paper and roll cake up in towel, starting with short end. Cool on a wire rack.

Meanwhile, beat the first five filling ingredients in a mixing bowl until soft peaks form. Unroll cake; spread with half the filling. Roll up. Spread remaining filling over cake. Sprinkle with cinnamon if desired. Store in the refrigerator. **Yield:** 10 servings.

Blueberry Cream Nut Roll

Schelby Thompson, Winter Haven, Florida

(Pictured below and on page 80)

For a special occasion or family treat during blueberry season, try this wonderful dessert. Don't let the recipe's length put you off—it's not complicated.

> 6 eggs, *separated*
> 3/4 cup sugar, *divided*
> 1-1/3 cups ground walnuts
> 1 teaspoon baking powder
> 1/2 teaspoon ground cinnamon
> 1/8 teaspoon salt

FILLING:

> 1 cup whipping cream
> 1/4 cup confectioners' sugar
> 1/2 teaspoon vanilla extract
> 1-1/2 cups fresh blueberries
> Additional confectioners' sugar and blueberries

In a mixing bowl, beat egg yolks for 1 minute. Add 1/2 cup sugar; beat until thick and lemon-colored. In a small bowl, combine walnuts, baking powder and cinnamon; fold into yolk mixture. In another mixing bowl, beat egg whites and salt until soft peaks form; gradually beat in remaining sugar until stiff peaks form. Fold a small amount of egg white mixture into nut mixture; gradually fold in remaining egg whites.

Line a greased 15-in. x 10-in. x 1-in. baking pan with waxed paper; grease and flour the paper. Spread batter evenly into pan. Bake at 350° for 20-25 minutes or until lightly browned. Cool in pan for 5 minutes. Turn onto a kitchen towel dusted with confectioners' sugar. Gently peel off waxed paper. Roll up in towel, jelly-roll style, starting with a long side. Cool on a wire rack.

For filling, whip the cream, sugar and vanilla; set aside 1/2 cup for garnish. Unroll cake; spread with remaining filling. Sprinkle with blueberries. Roll up; cover and refrigerate until serving. Dust with confectioners' sugar; garnish with blueberries and reserved whipped topping. **Yield:** 10-12 servings.

Editor's Note: This recipe does not contain flour.

Butter Pecan Ice Cream Roll

Elaine Hefner, Elida, Ohio

An active mother of four sons, I rely on recipes that keep entertaining simple. This cake roll can be chilling in the freezer long before guests arrive.

> 4 eggs
> 2 teaspoons baking powder
> 1/2 teaspoon salt
> 1 cup sugar
> 1/4 cup water
> 2 teaspoons vanilla extract
> 1 cup all-purpose flour

1-1/2 quarts butter pecan ice cream, softened
Confectioners' sugar and pecan halves, optional

In a mixing bowl, beat eggs, baking powder and salt until thick and lemon-colored. Gradually add sugar, beating until thickened. Beat in water and vanilla. Gradually add the flour.

Spread into a greased and waxed paper-lined 15-in. x 10-in. x 1-in. baking pan. Bake at 375° for 12-14 minutes or until cake is lightly browned. Cool for 5 minutes; turn onto a kitchen towel dusted with confectioners' sugar. Peel off waxed paper and roll up jelly-roll style, starting with a short side; cool on a wire rack.

When cool, unroll cake. Spread with ice cream to within 1 in. of edges. Reroll; cover and freeze until firm. May be frozen for up to 2 months. If desired, dust with confectioners' sugar and decorate with pecans before serving. **Yield:** 10 servings.

Prize-Winning Jelly Roll

Linda Andersen, Karlstad, Minnesota

(Pictured above and on page 80)

Twice I've won first place at our county fair with this recipe. I enjoy trying new recipes and cooking for my family and guests.

1-1/4 cups cake flour
1-1/2 cups sugar, *divided*
  1/2 teaspoon baking powder
    6 eggs, *separated*
    1 teaspoon cream of tartar
  1/2 teaspoon salt
  1/4 cup water
    1 teaspoon vanilla extract
    1 teaspoon lemon extract
Confectioners' sugar
    1 jar (12 ounces) strawberry, raspberry *or* currant jelly

In a bowl, combine cake flour, 1 cup sugar and baking powder; set aside. In a mixing bowl, beat the egg whites, cream of tartar and salt until soft peaks form. Add remaining sugar, 1 tablespoon at a time, beating well after each addition. Beat until stiff peaks form; set aside. In another mixing bowl, combine the egg yolks, water and extracts; mix well. Add dry ingredients; beat on medium for 1 minute. Gently fold in egg white mixture.

Line a greased 15-in. x 10-in. x 1-in. baking pan with waxed paper; spread batter into pan. Bake at 350° for 15-18 minutes or until cake springs back when lightly touched. Turn onto a kitchen towel dusted with confectioners' sugar; remove waxed paper. Roll cake up, starting with a short side; cool. Unroll cake; spread evenly with jelly. Roll up; dust with confectioners' sugar. **Yield:** 8-10 servings.

Pecan Cake Roll

Shirley Awald, Walkerton, Indiana

I'm a retired teacher. This dessert always went over big when I'd share it in the teachers' lounge!

    4 eggs, *separated*
    1 cup confectioners' sugar
    2 cups ground pecans
    1 cup whipping cream
    3 tablespoons sugar
    2 teaspoons baking cocoa
  1/2 teaspoon vanilla extract
Chocolate shavings and additional confectioners' sugar

In a mixing bowl, beat egg yolks and confectioners' sugar until thick, about 5 minutes. In another bowl, beat whites until soft peaks form; fold into yolk mixture. Fold in pecans until well blended (batter will be thin).

Grease a 15-in. x 10-in. x 1-in. baking pan; line with waxed paper and grease and flour paper. Spread batter into pan. Bake at 375° for 10-15 minutes or until cake springs back when lightly touched. Turn onto a kitchen towel dusted with confectioners' sugar. Peel off paper and roll cake up in towel, starting with short end. Cool on wire rack 1 hour.

Meanwhile, beat the cream, sugar, cocoa and vanilla in a mixing bowl until soft peaks form. Carefully unroll cake. Spread filling over cake; roll up again. Refrigerate. Garnish with chocolate shavings and confectioners' sugar. **Yield:** 10-12 servings.

Editor's Note: This cake does not contain flour.

Ice Cream Cake Roll

Kathy Scott, Hemingford, Nebraska

(Pictured below and on page 80)

This cake roll can be made and filled ahead of time, then thawed. Use whatever ice cream you have on hand.

    4 eggs, *separated*
    3/4 cup sugar
    1 teaspoon vanilla extract
    3/4 cup cake flour
    1/4 cup baking cocoa
    3/4 teaspoon baking powder
    1/4 teaspoon salt
    3 cups ice cream, softened
CHOCOLATE SAUCE:
    2 squares (1 ounce *each*) unsweetened
        baking chocolate
    1/4 cup butter *or* margarine
    2/3 cup evaporated milk, heated to 160° to 170°
    1 cup sugar

In a large mixing bowl, beat egg yolks on high for 3 minutes or until light and fluffy. Gradually add sugar and vanilla, beating until thick and lemon-colored. Combine flour, cocoa and baking powder; gradually add to egg yolk mixture. Beat on low until well mixed (mixture will be thick). Beat egg whites and salt until soft peaks form. Fold a small amount into batter until no streaks of white remain; add the remaining egg whites.

Grease a 15-in. x 10-in. x 1-in. pan; line with waxed paper and grease and flour paper. Spread batter evenly in pan. Bake at 350° for 15 minutes or until cake springs back when lightly touched. Turn out onto a kitchen towel dusted with confectioners' sugar. Peel off paper and roll up in towel. Cool for 30 minutes.

Unroll cake; spread with ice cream to within 1 in. of edges. Roll up again. Cover with plastic wrap and freeze until serving. In the top of a double boiler over hot water, melt chocolate and butter. Gradually add warm milk and sugar; stir constantly for 5 minutes or until completely dissolved. Spoon over slices of cake. **Yield:** 10 servings (1-1/2 cups sauce).

Pumpkin Cake Roll

June Mullins, Livonia, Missouri

(Pictured above)

Roll out this well-rounded dessert and get set to harvest plenty of compliments. It earns me rave reviews whenever I serve it.

    3 eggs
    1 cup sugar
    2/3 cup canned pumpkin
    3/4 cup biscuit/baking mix
    2 teaspoons ground cinnamon
    1 teaspoon pumpkin pie spice
    1/2 teaspoon ground nutmeg
    1 cup chopped nuts
Confectioners' sugar
FILLING:
    2 packages (3 ounces *each*) cream cheese,
        softened
    1/4 cup butter *or* margarine, softened
    1 cup confectioners' sugar
    1 teaspoon vanilla extract

In a mixing bowl, beat eggs. Gradually add sugar. Stir in pumpkin; mix well. Combine the biscuit mix, cinnamon, pie spice and nutmeg. Add to egg mixture; mix well.

Line a 15-in. x 10-in. x 1-in. pan with waxed paper; grease and flour the paper. Spread batter evenly in pan. Sprinkle with nuts. Bake at 375° for 13-15 minutes or until a toothpick inserted near the center comes out clean. Cool for 10 minutes.

Turn cake onto a kitchen towel dusted with confectioners' sugar. Remove paper; roll up cake in towel, starting with a short side. Cool on a wire rack.

For filling, in a mixing bowl, beat cream cheese, butter, sugar and vanilla until smooth. Unroll cake. Spread filling over cake to within 1 in. of edges. Gently roll up; place seam side down on a platter. Refrigerate until serving. **Yield:** 10 servings.

p. 90

p. 93

p. 92

p. 96

p. 94

Clockwise from top left: Kitty Cat Cupcakes, Cream-Filled Cupcakes, Caramel Apple Cupcakes, Cupcake Cones and Chocolate Cherry Cupcakes.

Cupcakes

Kitty Cat Cupcakes

Doris Barb, El Dorado, Kansas

(Pictured above and on page 88)

On a bake sale table or alone at home, these feline treats won't last nine lives! The cute candy faces will catch attention fast…and the tasty orange-coconut cake will have folks snatching seconds.

   2/3 cup shortening
1-3/4 cups sugar, *divided*
   4 eggs, *separated*
2-1/2 cups all-purpose flour
2-1/2 teaspoons baking powder
   1/2 teaspoon salt
   1 cup orange juice
   1 cup flaked coconut
FROSTING:
1-1/4 cups sugar
   1/4 cup water
   1/4 cup light corn syrup
   1/8 teaspoon salt
   1 egg white
   5 large marshmallows, quartered
   1/2 teaspoon vanilla extract
Assorted M&M's
   1 piece red shoestring licorice, cut into
      3/4-inch pieces
Chocolate sprinkles
About 9 vanilla wafers
   2 cups flaked coconut, toasted

In a mixing bowl, cream shortening and 1-1/2 cups sugar. Add egg yolks; mix well. Combine the flour, baking powder and salt; add to creamed mixture alternately with orange juice.

In a small mixing bowl, beat egg whites until soft peaks form. Gradually add the remaining sugar. Fold into creamed mixture with coconut. Fill paper-lined muffin cups two-thirds full. Bake at 350° for 15 minutes or until a toothpick inserted near the center comes out clean. Cool for 5 minutes before removing from pans to wire racks to cool completely.

For frosting, in a saucepan, combine the sugar, water, corn syrup and salt. Cook, without stirring, over medium heat until a candy thermometer reads 234° (soft-ball stage). Meanwhile, in a small mixing bowl, beat egg white until stiff peaks form. Beat in hot syrup mixture. Add marshmallows and vanilla; beat until stiff peaks form. Frost cupcakes.

Arrange M&M's for eyes and nose, shoestring licorice for mouth and chocolate sprinkles for whiskers. For ears, cut wafers into quarters with a serrated knife; place two on each cupcake, rounded side down. Sprinkle with coconut. Refrigerate until serving. **Yield:** about 1-1/2 dozen.

From Cakes to Cupcakes

MOST cake batters can be baked in paper-lined muffin cups. A one-layer cake recipe yields 12-15 cupcakes; a two-layer cake recipe yields 24-30 cupcakes.

Spice Cupcakes

Carla Hodenfield, New Town, North Dakota

(Pictured below)

These moist spicy cupcakes with creamy caramel frosting are a delicious treat. The recipe has been in my family for years. When I was growing up, it seemed these cupcakes were always on hand.

    2 cups water
    1 cup raisins
    1/2 cup shortening
    1 cup sugar
    1 egg
1-3/4 cups all-purpose flour
    1 teaspoon baking soda
    1/2 teaspoon salt
    1/2 teaspoon *each* ground allspice, cloves,
        cinnamon and nutmeg
    1/4 cup chopped walnuts
FROSTING:
    1 cup packed brown sugar
    1/3 cup half-and-half cream
    1/4 teaspoon salt
    3 tablespoons butter *or* margarine
    1 teaspoon vanilla extract
1-1/4 cups confectioners' sugar
Coarsely chopped walnuts, optional

In a saucepan, bring water and raisins to a boil. Reduce heat; simmer for 10 minutes. Remove from heat and set aside (do not drain). In a mixing bowl, cream shortening and sugar. Add egg and raisins. Combine dry ingredients; add to creamed mixture and mix well. Stir in walnuts. Fill greased or paper-lined muffin cups with 1/3 cup batter each. Bake at 350° for 20-25 minutes or until a toothpick inserted near the center comes out clean. Cool for 10 minutes; remove from pan to a wire rack.

For frosting, combine brown sugar, cream and salt in a saucepan. Bring to a boil over medium-low heat;

cook and stir until smooth. Stir in butter and vanilla. Remove from heat; cool slightly. Stir in confectioners' sugar until smooth. Frost cupcakes; top with nuts if desired. Store in the refrigerator. **Yield:** 14 cupcakes.

Chocolate Caramel Cupcakes

Bev Spain, Bellville, Ohio

(Pictured above)

A few baking staples are all you need to throw together these chewy delights. Boxed cake mix and a can of frosting make them fast, but caramel, walnuts and chocolate chips tucked inside make them memorable. We like them with ice cream.

    1 package (18-1/4 ounces) chocolate cake mix
    24 caramels
    3/4 cup semisweet chocolate chips
    1 cup chopped walnuts
Chocolate frosting
Additional walnuts, optional

Prepare cake batter according to package directions. Fill 24 greased or paper-lined muffin cups one-third full; set remaining batter aside. Bake at 350° for 7-8 minutes or until top of cupcake appears set.

Gently press a caramel into each cupcake; sprinkle with chocolate chips and walnuts. Top with remaining batter. Bake 15-20 minutes longer or until a toothpick inserted near the center of cake comes out clean. Cool for 5 minutes; remove from pans to wire racks to cool completely. Frost with chocolate frosting. Sprinkle with additional nuts if desired. **Yield:** 2 dozen.

Editor's Note: This recipe was tested with Betty Crocker cake mix and Hershey caramels.

Caramel Apple Cupcakes

Diane Halferty, Corpus Christi, Texas

(Pictured below and on page 88)

Bring these extra-special cupcakes to your next bake sale and watch how quickly they disappear—if your family doesn't gobble them up first! Kids will go for the fun appearance and tasty toppings while adults will appreciate the moist spiced cake underneath.

>   1 package (18-1/4 ounces) spice *or* carrot
>   cake mix
>   2 cups chopped peeled tart apples
>   20 caramels*
>   3 tablespoons milk
>   1 cup finely chopped pecans, toasted
>   12 Popsicle sticks

Prepare cake batter according to package directions; fold in apples. Fill 12 greased or paper-lined jumbo muffin cups three-fourths full. Bake at 350° for 20 minutes or until a toothpick inserted near the center comes out clean. Cool for 10 minutes before removing from pans to wire racks to cool completely.

In a saucepan, cook the caramels and milk over low heat until smooth. Spread over cupcakes. Sprinkle with pecans. Insert a wooden stick into the center of each cupcake. **Yield:** 1 dozen.

*Editor's Note: This recipe was tested with Hershey caramels.

Rosy Rhubarb Cupcakes

Sharon Nichols, Brookings, South Dakota

If you're in a hurry, these are good even without frosting. The recipe works well with either fresh or frozen rhubarb, and a hint of nutmeg sparks the flavor.

>   1/2 cup shortening
>   1 cup packed brown sugar
>   1/2 cup sugar
>   1 egg
>   2 cups all-purpose flour
>   1 teaspoon baking soda
>   1/4 teaspoon ground nutmeg
>   1 cup buttermilk
> 1-1/2 cups finely chopped fresh *or* frozen rhubarb,
>   thawed
> **Cream cheese frosting, optional**

In a mixing bowl, cream shortening and sugars. Add egg and mix well. Combine flour, baking soda and nutmeg; add to creamed mixture alternately with buttermilk. Fold in the rhubarb. Fill paper-lined muffin cups two-thirds full. Bake at 350° for 30-35 minutes or until a toothpick inserted near the center comes out clean. Frost if desired. **Yield:** about 1-1/2 dozen.

pans to wire racks to cool completely.

In a mixing bowl, combine butter, shortening, confectioners' sugar, milk, vanilla and salt; beat until fluffy, about 5 minutes. Insert a very small tip into a pastry or plastic bag; fill with cream filling. Push the tip through the bottom of paper liner to fill each cupcake. Frost tops with chocolate frosting. **Yield:** 3 dozen.

St. Patrick's Day Cupcakes

Kathy Meyer, Almond, Wisconsin

(Pictured below)

These stir-and-bake cupcakes go together super-quick. Pistachio pudding mix gives them a mild flavor and pretty pastel color that makes them perfect for St. Patrick's Day.

1-3/4 cups all-purpose flour
  2/3 cup sugar
    1 package (3.4 ounces) instant pistachio
      pudding mix
    2 teaspoons baking powder
  1/2 teaspoon salt
    2 eggs
1-1/4 cups milk
  1/2 cup vegetable oil
    1 teaspoon vanilla extract
Green food coloring, optional
Cream cheese frosting

In a bowl, combine the dry ingredients. In another bowl, beat eggs, milk, oil and vanilla; add to dry ingredients and mix until blended. Fill paper-lined muffin cups three-fourths full. Bake at 375° for 18-22 minutes or until a toothpick inserted in the center comes out clean. Cool on a wire rack. If desired, add food coloring to frosting. Frost cupcakes. Store in the refrigerator. **Yield:** 1 dozen.

Cream-Filled Cupcakes

Edie DeSpain, Logan, Utah

(Pictured above and on page 88)

Folks who enjoy homemade chocolate cupcakes are even more impressed when they bite into these treats and find a fluffy cream filling. These are great in a lunch box or on a buffet table.

    3 cups all-purpose flour
    2 cups sugar
  1/3 cup baking cocoa
    2 teaspoons baking soda
    1 teaspoon salt
    2 eggs
    1 cup milk
    1 cup vegetable oil
    1 cup water
    1 teaspoon vanilla extract
FILLING:
  1/4 cup butter *or* margarine, softened
  1/4 cup shortening
    2 cups confectioners' sugar
    3 tablespoons milk
    1 teaspoon vanilla extract
Pinch salt
Chocolate frosting

In a mixing bowl, combine the first five ingredients. Add eggs, milk, oil, water and vanilla. Beat until smooth, about 2 minutes. Fill paper-lined muffin cups half full. Bake at 375° for 15-20 minutes or until a toothpick inserted near the center comes out clean. Remove from

Cupcake Cones

Mina Dyck, Boissevain, Manitoba

(Pictured above and on page 88)

Children love this treat, which is not as messy as a piece of cake. They're fun to make and eat!

1/3 cup butter *or* margarine, softened
1/2 cup creamy peanut butter
1-1/2 cups packed brown sugar
  2 eggs
  1 teaspoon vanilla extract
  2 cups all-purpose flour
2-1/2 teaspoons baking powder
  1/2 teaspoon salt
  3/4 cup milk
Cake ice cream cones (about 3 inches tall)
Frosting of your choice
Sprinkles *or* chopped peanuts, optional

In a mixing bowl, cream butter, peanut butter and brown sugar. Beat in eggs and vanilla. Combine dry ingredients; add to creamed mixture alternately with milk. Place ice cream cones in muffin cups. Spoon about 3 tablespoons batter into each cone, filling to 3/4 in. from the top. Bake at 350° for 25-30 minutes or until a toothpick inserted near the center comes out clean. Frost and decorate as desired. **Yield:** about 2 dozen.

Cream Cheese Cupcakes

Nancy Reichert, Thomasville, Georgia

It's hard to believe these cupcakes can taste so delicious, yet be so easy. Frost them if you wish, but my family likes them plain.

  1 package (3 ounces) cream cheese, softened
  1 package (18-1/4 ounces) yellow cake mix
1-1/4 cups water

1/2 cup butter *or* margarine, melted
  3 eggs
Chocolate frosting, optional

In a mixing bowl, beat cream cheese until smooth. Add cake mix, water, butter and eggs; mix well. Spoon batter by 1/4 cupfuls into paper-lined muffin cups. Bake at 350° for 25 minutes or until golden. Remove to a wire rack to cool completely. Frost if desired. Store in the refrigerator. **Yield:** 2 dozen.

Carrot Cupcakes

Doreen Kelly, Roslyn, Pennsylvania

(Pictured below)

To try to get my family to eat more vegetables, I often "hide" nutritional foods inside sweet treats. The carrots add wonderful moistness to these cupcakes.

  4 eggs
  2 cups sugar
  1 cup vegetable oil
  2 cups all-purpose flour
  2 teaspoons ground cinnamon
  1 teaspoon baking soda
  1 teaspoon baking powder
  1 teaspoon ground allspice
1/2 teaspoon salt
  3 cups grated carrots
CHUNKY FROSTING:
  1 package (8 ounces) cream cheese, softened
1/4 cup butter *or* margarine, softened
  2 cups confectioners' sugar
1/2 cup flaked coconut
1/2 cup chopped pecans
1/2 cup chopped raisins

In a mixing bowl, beat eggs, sugar and oil. Combine the flour, cinnamon, baking soda, baking powder, allspice and salt; gradually add to egg mixture. Stir in carrots. Fill greased or paper-lined muffin cups two-thirds full. Bake at 325° for 20-25 minutes or until a toothpick inserted near the center comes out clean. Cool for 5 min-

utes before removing from pans to wire racks.

For frosting, in a mixing bowl, beat cream cheese and butter until combined. Gradually beat in confectioners' sugar. Stir in coconut, pecans and raisins. Frost cupcakes. Store in the refrigerator. **Yield:** 2 dozen.

per-lined miniature muffin cups. Top with about 1 teaspoon of filling. Bake at 350° for 18-23 minutes or until a toothpick inserted in chocolate portion comes out clean. Cool for 10 minutes; remove to wire racks to cool completely. Store in the refrigerator. **Yield:** 6 dozen.

Chocolate-Bottom Mini-Cupcakes

Bertille Cooper, St. Inigoes, Maryland

These freeze very well. I like to keep a batch on hand for drop-in guests or when I'm too busy to bake.

FILLING:
    1 package (8 ounces) cream cheese, softened
    1 egg
    1/3 cup sugar
    1/8 teaspoon salt
    1 cup (6 ounces) semisweet chocolate chips
BATTER:
    1 cup water
    1/3 cup vegetable oil
    1 tablespoon vinegar
    1 teaspoon vanilla extract
1-1/2 cups all-purpose flour
    1 cup sugar
    1/4 cup baking cocoa
    1 teaspoon baking soda
    1 teaspoon salt

In a mixing bowl, beat cream cheese, egg, sugar and salt until smooth. Stir in chocolate chips; set aside. For batter, combine water, oil, vinegar and vanilla in another mixing bowl. Combine remaining ingredients; add to the liquid mixture and beat well (batter will be thin). Spoon about 2 teaspoons of batter into greased or pa-

Peanut Butter Cup Cupcakes

Heidi Harrington, Steuben, Maine

(Pictured above)

Kids love these rich, yummy cupcakes in school lunches or at parties. They're so easy to make.

    1/3 cup shortening
    1/3 cup peanut butter
1-1/4 cups packed brown sugar
    2 eggs
    1 teaspoon vanilla extract
1-3/4 cups all-purpose flour
1-3/4 teaspoons baking powder
    1 teaspoon salt
    1 cup milk
  16 miniature peanut butter cups

In a mixing bowl, cream the shortening, peanut butter and brown sugar. Add eggs and vanilla; mix well. Combine flour, baking powder and salt; add to creamed mixture alternately with milk.

Fill paper-lined muffin cups with 1/4 cup of batter. Press a peanut butter cup into the center of each until top edge is even with batter. Bake at 350° for 22-24 minutes or until a toothpick inserted on an angle toward the center comes out clean. **Yield:** 16 cupcakes.

Mocha Cupcakes

Lorna Smith, New Hazelton, British Columbia

(Pictured below)

This recipe is one that I have called on over the years for numerous occasions—birthdays, PTA meetings, for serving to company, etc. Everyone likes it.

> 1 cup boiling water
> 1 cup mayonnaise*
> 1 teaspoon vanilla extract
> 2 cups all-purpose flour
> 1 cup sugar
> 1/2 cup baking cocoa
> 2 teaspoons baking soda

MOCHA FROSTING:
> 3/4 cup confectioners' sugar
> 1/4 cup baking cocoa
> 1/2 to 1 teaspoon instant coffee granules

Pinch salt
1-1/2 cups whipping cream

In a mixing bowl, combine water, mayonnaise and vanilla. Combine flour, sugar, cocoa and baking soda; add to the mayonnaise mixture and beat until well mixed. Fill greased or paper-lined muffin cups two-thirds full. Bake at 350° for 20-25 minutes or until a toothpick inserted near the center comes out clean. Cool in tins 10 minutes; remove to wire racks and cool completely.

For frosting, combine sugar, cocoa, coffee and salt in a mixing bowl. Stir in cream; cover and chill with beaters for 30 minutes. Beat frosting until stiff peaks form. Frost the cupcakes. Store in the refrigerator. **Yield:** about 1-1/2 dozen.

To make a cake: Prepare batter and bake as directed for cupcakes, except use two greased 8-in. round baking pans. Frost between layers and sides and top of cake. Serves 12.

*Editor's Note: Reduced-fat or fat-free mayonnaise may not be substituted for regular mayonnaise.

Chocolate Cherry Cupcakes

Bertille Cooper, St. Inigoes, Maryland

(Pictured above and on page 88)

Inside each of these chocolate cupcakes is a fruity surprise! I start with a convenient cake mix to produce my special treats.

> 1 package (18-1/4 ounces) chocolate cake mix
> 1-1/3 cups water
> 1/2 cup vegetable oil
> 3 eggs
> 1 can (21 ounces) cherry pie filling
> 1 can (16 ounces) vanilla frosting

In a mixing bowl, combine cake mix, water, oil and eggs; mix well. Spoon batter by 1/4 cupfuls into paper-lined muffin cups. Spoon a rounded teaspoon of pie filling onto the center of each cupcake. Set remaining pie filling aside. Bake at 350° for 20-25 minutes or until a toothpick inserted on an angle toward the center comes out clean. Remove to a wire rack to cool completely.

Frost cupcakes; top with one cherry from pie filling. Serve additional pie filling with cupcakes or refrigerate for another use. **Yield:** 2 dozen.

Frosting Cupcakes...Fast

CUPCAKES can quickly be frosted by dipping the top of each cupcake in frosting; turn slightly and remove.

Coconut Orange Cupcakes

Donna Justin, Sparta, Wisconsin

This tried-and-true recipe features the delicate tastes of orange, white chocolate and coconut in an easy dessert worthy of company. It yields 2 dozen delicious cupcakes with a pretty topping.

    1 cup sugar
  2/3 cup vegetable oil
    2 eggs
    1 cup orange juice
    3 cups all-purpose flour
    1 tablespoon baking powder
    1 teaspoon baking soda
  3/4 teaspoon salt
    1 can (11 ounces) mandarin oranges,
        drained
    1 cup vanilla chips
TOPPING:
    1 cup flaked coconut
  1/3 cup sugar
    2 tablespoons butter *or* margarine, melted

In a mixing bowl, combine the sugar, oil, eggs and orange juice; mix well. Combine dry ingredients; stir into orange juice mixture just until moistened. Fold in oranges and chips.

Fill greased or paper-lined muffin cups two-thirds full. Combine topping ingredients; sprinkle over cupcakes. Bake at 375° for 15-20 minutes or until golden brown. **Yield:** 2 dozen.

Lemon Cream Cupcakes

Ruth Ann Stelfox, Raymond, Alberta

(Pictured below)

Just thinking of these delicate cupcakes makes me hungry! I'm sure your family will love them, too.

    1 cup butter *or* margarine, softened
    2 cups sugar
    3 eggs
    2 teaspoons grated lemon peel
    1 teaspoon vanilla extract
3-1/2 cups all-purpose flour
    2 teaspoons baking powder
    1 teaspoon baking soda
  1/2 teaspoon salt
    2 cups (16 ounces) sour cream
FROSTING:
    3 tablespoons butter *or* margarine, softened
2-1/4 cups confectioners' sugar
    2 tablespoons lemon juice
  3/4 teaspoon vanilla extract
  1/4 teaspoon grated lemon peel
    1 to 2 tablespoons milk

In a mixing bowl, cream butter and sugar. Beat in eggs, one at a time. Add lemon peel and vanilla; mix well. Combine dry ingredients; add to creamed mixture alternately with sour cream (batter will be thick). Fill greased or paper-lined muffin cups with 1/4 cup of batter. Bake at 350° for 25-30 minutes or until a toothpick inserted near the center comes out clean. Cool for 10 minutes; remove to wire racks to cool completely.

For frosting, cream butter and sugar in a mixing bowl. Add lemon juice, vanilla, peel and milk; beat until smooth. Frost cupcakes. Store in the refrigerator. **Yield:** about 2-1/2 dozen.

p. 106

p. 108

p. 104

TIME OUT FOR A BIRTHDAY PARTY

p. 100

p. 106

Clockwise from top left: Happy Clown Cake, Buggy Gal Birthday Cake, Football Cake, Dump Truck Cake and Puppy Dog Cake.

Kids' Birthday Cakes

Puppy Dog Cake

Nancy Reichert, Thomasville, Georgia

(Pictured above and on page 98)

No bones about it—just a glance at this tasty canine confection is bound to get guests' stomachs growling! The birthday dessert is surprisingly simple to prepare, too…beginning with a mouth-watering coconut cake recipe. You can easily "groom" Nancy's baked treat into a pooch like our Test Kitchen did by adding chocolate, candy and a fruit snack to make a friendly face.

> 5 squares (1 ounce *each*) semisweet chocolate
> 2 tablespoons plus 1-1/2 teaspoons corn syrup

CAKE:

> 4 squares (1 ounce *each*) white baking chocolate
> 1/2 cup water
> 1 cup butter (no substitutes), softened
> 2 cups sugar
> 4 eggs, *separated*
> 3 teaspoons vanilla extract
> 2-1/2 cups all-purpose flour

> 1 teaspoon baking soda
> 1 cup buttermilk
> 1 cup flaked coconut
> 1 cup chopped pecans

FROSTING:

> 1 package (8 ounces) cream cheese, softened
> 1/2 cup butter (no substitutes), softened
> 3-3/4 cups confectioners' sugar
> 1 tablespoon milk
> 1 teaspoon vanilla extract

DECORATION:

> 4 chocolate-covered peppermint candies
> 1 piece black shoestring licorice (4 inches)
> 1 red fruit roll-up

In a microwave-safe bowl, melt the semisweet chocolate; stir until smooth. Stir in corn syrup just until mixture is well blended, forms a ball and is no longer shiny. Turn onto an 8-in. square of waxed paper. Press chocolate mixture into a 7-in. square. Let the mixture stand at room temperature until dry to the touch, about 2 hours.

Roll out chocolate mixture on waxed paper to 1/8-in. thickness. Using a sharp knife, cut out two 4-in. x 2-in. ears; round one end of each. Cut out two 1-1/4-in. circles for eyes, two 1-in.-long strips for eyebrows and one 5-in. heart for muzzle; set aside.

In a microwave-safe bowl, heat white chocolate and water until chocolate is melted; cool. In a large mixing bowl, cream butter and sugar. Beat in egg yolks, vanilla and cooled white chocolate mixture. Combine flour and baking soda; add to the creamed mixture alternately with buttermilk. In a small mixing bowl, beat egg whites until stiff peaks form. Fold into the white chocolate mixture with coconut and pecans.

Fill four greased muffin cups half full with batter. Spoon remaining batter into two greased 9-in. round baking pans. Bake cupcakes at 350° for 15 minutes and cakes for 35 minutes or until a toothpick comes out clean. Cool cupcakes for 5 minutes and cakes for 10 minutes before removing from pans to wire racks to cool completely.

For frosting, in a mixing bowl, beat cream cheese and butter. Add confectioners' sugar, milk and vanilla. Set aside 1 teaspoon for decorating.

To assemble, place one cake on a 14-in. x 11-in. covered board. Cut off cupcake tops; cut a 1/4-in. rounded portion off one edge of each. Place cutout portion of two cupcakes against side of cake with edges touching; frost top of cake and cupcakes. Top with remaining cake and cupcakes; frost top and sides.

Place ears opposite the cupcakes, inserting the flat ends into side of the cake 1/4 in. from top. Fold ears over the top of cake. Position eyes, eyebrows and muzzle as shown in photo at left.

Place a small amount of reserved frosting on the back of each mint; insert two for eyes and two for nose. Place licorice on the muzzle as shown. With scissors, cut fruit roll-up into a 4-in. strip and round one end; place straight end under muzzle for tongue. Store in the refrigerator. **Yield:** 10-12 servings.

Play Ball Cake

Sue Gronholz, Columbus, Wisconsin

(Pictured at right)

You won't need any fancy pans for this sporting dessert, which was the centerpiece of a baseball theme party we hosted a while ago. Our kids and their cousins all wanted pieces that had the red licorice "lacing"! By the way, I have found that fresh, pliable licorice works the best for forming the laces on the curved ball cake.

1/2 cup shortening
1-1/2 cups sugar
  2 eggs
  1 teaspoon vanilla extract
2-1/2 cups cake flour
  2 teaspoons baking powder
1/2 teaspoon salt
  1 cup milk
FROSTING:
  1/2 cup shortening
  1/2 cup butter *or* margarine, softened

3 cups confectioners' sugar
4 tablespoons milk, *divided*
1/2 teaspoon vanilla extract
1/4 teaspoon almond extract
Dash salt
  1/4 cup baking cocoa
Red shoestring licorice

In a mixing bowl, cream shortening and sugar. Add eggs, one at a time, beating well after each. Add vanilla. Combine flour, baking powder and salt; add alternately with milk to the creamed mixture. Pour 1-1/2 cups batter into a greased and floured 3-cup ovenproof bowl. Pour remaining batter into a greased and floured 9-in. round baking pan. Bake at 325° for 40-45 minutes or until a toothpick comes out clean. Cool for 10 minutes; remove to a wire rack to cool completely.

For frosting, beat shortening and butter in a mixing bowl. Add sugar, 3 tablespoons milk, extracts and salt; beat until smooth. Set aside 1 cup. To remaining frosting, beat in cocoa and remaining milk.

Cut a 3-in. x 1-in. oval for the thumb opening from an edge of the 9-in. cake. Place cake on an 11-in. covered board. Frost with chocolate frosting. With four pieces of licorice, form two crosses over thumb opening for laces in mitt. Frost the rounded cake with white frosting. Use licorice pieces to form laces of ball. Place on mitt cake opposite the thumb opening. **Yield:** 8-10 servings.

Firecracker Cake

N. and C. Linden, Naperville, Illinois

(Pictured below)

Spark "oohs" and "aahs" at your next birthday event with this delicious dazzler. It's sure to fire up taste buds! The dandy dessert takes off thanks to moist cake bursting with lemon flavor shared by the Lindens. Our Test Kitchen staff came up with the colorful home-made frosting, which forms the eye-catching firecrackers. As a grand finale, you can top your confection with a cream-filled snack cake and cover it with more icing to make an extra-large sparkler.

3/4 cup butter *or* margarine, softened
1-1/4 cups sugar
    8 egg yolks
2-1/2 cups all-purpose flour
    3 teaspoons baking powder
    1/4 teaspoon salt
    3/4 cup milk
    1 teaspoon vanilla extract
    1 teaspoon lemon juice
    1 teaspoon grated lemon peel
FROSTING:
    3/4 cup butter *or* margarine, softened
7-1/2 cups confectioners' sugar
    1/3 to 1/2 cup lemon juice
Red, blue and yellow gel *or* paste food coloring
    1 cream-filled sponge cake

In a large mixing bowl, cream the butter and sugar. In a small mixing bowl, beat egg yolks until light and lemon-colored; add to creamed mixture. Combine the flour, baking powder and salt; add to creamed mixture alternately with milk. Beat in the vanilla, lemon juice and peel.

Pour into two greased and floured 8-in. round baking pans. Bake at 325° for 20-25 minutes or until a toothpick inserted near the center of cakes comes out clean. Cool cakes for 10 minutes before removing from the pans to wire racks to cool completely.

For frosting, in a large mixing bowl, cream butter and confectioners' sugar. Add enough lemon juice to achieve desired consistency. Place 2/3 cup frosting each in two small bowls; tint one red and one blue. Place 1/3 cup frosting in another small bowl; tint yellow. Leave the remaining frosting white.

Using a serrated knife, level the top of each cake. Place one cake on a 10-in. round serving platter. Frost top of cake with white frosting; top with second cake. Spread top and sides with remaining white frosting.

Place each of the tinted frostings in pastry or plastic bags. Insert star tip #21. Alternating colors and using a rope pattern, pipe 12 firecrackers around side of cake. Pipe a yellow star on top of cake above firecrackers.

Place the cream-filled sponge cake centered on top of the cake. Alternating red and blue frosting, pipe diagonal stripes across the cream-filled sponge cake. Pipe a large yellow star above sponge cake. **Yield:** 12 servings.

2 burstin' berry-flavored Fruit Roll-Ups,*
  divided
5 uncooked spaghetti noodles
1 round wooden toothpick
1 butterscotch chip
1 miniature marshmallow

Prepare and bake cake according to package directions, using two greased and floured 9-in. round baking pans. Cool for 10 minutes; remove from pans to wire racks to cool completely.

For frosting, cream shortening, butter, sugar and vanilla in a mixing bowl. Gradually beat in milk until light and fluffy. Tint with green paste food coloring. Place cake on a serving platter or 10-in. round covered board; frost between layers and top and sides of cake.

Insert tip into pastry or plastic bag; fill with frosting. Pipe grass along bottom edge of cake.

Place coconut in a plastic bag; add 5-6 drops green liquid food coloring. Shake until color is evenly distributed. Set aside.

For the green, trace a 4-in. circle on waxed paper; cut out. Place on top of cake 1 in. from an edge. Sprinkle green coconut over the cake top; remove the waxed paper. Insert the chocolate kiss, point side down, into green for the hole.

For the pin, unroll one fruit roll-up. Cut a 2-1/4-in. x 2-in. x 1-in. triangle from the red portion; set aside the unused portion. Wrap shortest side of triangle around the end of one noodle. Insert noodle into the green next to the hole.

For the tee, gently insert toothpick into pointed end of butterscotch chip. Insert tee into cake opposite the pin. Place marshmallow on tee for the golf ball.

From the reserved roll-up, cut a 4-3/4-in. x 1/2-in. strip out of the red section for the golf bag strap; set blue portion aside. Unroll second roll-up; cut between blue and red portions. Roll up red portion into a 1-in.-diameter tube for the golf bag. Attach the strap to the side of bag. Fold the ends over top and bottom of bag, leaving a 1-in. loop near the top for the handle; set aside.

For golf clubs, break the remaining noodles into 4-in., 5-in. and 6-in. pieces. Cut the blue portions of roll-ups into eight 2-1/2-in. x 1/2-in. strips. Mold each strip around one end of a noodle, forming a club head. Stand the golf bag near the tee. Place golf clubs in the bag and gently press bag into the cake. **Yield:** 8 servings.

*Editor's Note: This recipe was tested with Betty Crocker brand Fun 'n' Games Fruit Roll-Ups. Any two-color roll-up can be used.

Hole in One Cake

(Pictured above)

One things's for sure…golfers won't be afraid of a "slice" on this course. On the contrary—they'll want to cut a big wedge of the cake designed by our Test Kitchen staff. The chocolate cake—made with a purchased mix—sports a fairway and green groomed with bright frosting and colored coconut. Then noodles, fruit snacks and other sweets "equip" the scene with a golf bag, pin and more. Game to try it yourself? Just follow the easy instructions provided here. It's sure to score a hole in one with any golfer you know!

    1 package (18-1/4 ounces) chocolate cake mix
1/2 cup shortening
1/2 cup butter *or* margarine, softened
    4 cups confectioners' sugar
    1 teaspoon vanilla extract
    3 tablespoons milk
Green paste and liquid food coloring
#233 multi-opening pastry tip *or* #2 round tip
Pastry bag *or* plastic bag with small hole cut in
  corner
1/2 cup flaked coconut
    1 miniature chocolate kiss

Keeping Cakes Fresh

KEEP CAKES fresh by investing in a cake cover or a covered cake carrier.

If you don't have a cake cover, stick toothpicks at 4-inch intervals in the top and sides of the cake; lightly drape a large sheet of plastic wrap over the picks.

Foil-covered heavy corrugated cardboard (12 inches x 7-1/2 inches)
Candy necklaces, foil-covered chocolate coins, candy pacifiers **or** candies of your choice
2 pieces berry tie-dye Fruit Roll-Ups

In two batches, prepare and bake cakes according to package directions, using two greased and floured 13-in. x 9-in. x 2-in. baking pans. Cool for 10 minutes; remove from pans to cool on wire racks.

In a large mixing bowl, cream butter; beat in chocolate, vanilla, confectioners' sugar and enough milk to achieve spreading consistency. Center one cake on a 16-in. x 12-in. covered board; frost top. Top with remaining cake; frost top and sides of cake. With a metal spatula, smooth frosting to resemble boards.

For chest lid, insert 4-in. skewers equally spaced 6 in. into one long side of corrugated cardboard lid. Frost top of lid. Cut a small hole in the corner of a pastry or plastic bag; insert star tip #21. Pipe a shell border on edges of lid and for handles on sides of chest.

Place one 7-1/2-in. skewer on each side of cake top, about 3-1/2 in. from back of chest. Position lid over cake; gently insert short skewers into cake about 1 in. from back of chest. Rest lid on long skewers.

Arrange candy of your choice in the chest. Cut a small keyhole from a fruit roll-up; center on front of cake. Position strips of fruit roll-ups in front and back of chest. **Yield:** 14-16 serving.

Football Cake

Ruth Andrewson, Leavenworth, Washington

(Pictured at right and on page 98)

Why not surprise your favorite football fan on his birthday with a cake he's bound to get a kick out of? The birthday dessert designed by our Test Kitchen begins with Ruth's chocolate cake recipe. Of course, this cake can cover the field for non-birthday occasions as well. Think what a hit it would be at a Super Bowl party… taken along for tailgating at a game in the fall…or at a school bake sale.

    1/2 cup boiling water
      1 bar (4 ounces) German sweet chocolate, chopped
      1 cup butter **or** margarine, softened
      2 cups sugar
      4 eggs, *separated*
      1 teaspoon vanilla extract
2-1/2 cups cake flour
      1 teaspoon baking soda
    1/2 teaspoon salt
      1 cup buttermilk
FROSTING/FILLING:
      1 cup sugar
      1 tablespoon cornstarch
      1 cup evaporated milk
      3 egg yolks, beaten
    1/2 cup butter **or** margarine, melted

Treasure Chest Birthday Cake

Sharon Hanson, Franklin, Tennessee

(Pictured above)

Swashbucklers of all ages were eager to seize a chocolaty piece of this birthday cake I served at my son's party a few years ago, although some guests thought it was too cute to cut! Folks were impressed with the edible pirate's treasure chest and loved the rich chocolate icing. It was fun to make and even more fun to eat!

      2 packages (18-1/4 ounces *each*) chocolate cake mix
1-1/3 cups butter **or** margarine, softened
      8 squares (1 ounce *each*) unsweetened chocolate, melted and cooled
      6 teaspoons vanilla extract
7-1/2 to 8 cups confectioners' sugar
    1/3 to 1/2 cup milk
      5 wooden skewers (three 4 inches, two 7-1/2 inches)

1 teaspoon vanilla extract
2-1/2 cups flaked coconut
Green food coloring
1 can (16 ounces) vanilla frosting
2 tablespoons baking cocoa
6 white pipe cleaners

In a small bowl, pour water over chocolate; set aside. In a mixing bowl, cream butter and sugar. Add egg yolks, one at a time, beating well after each. Add cooled chocolate and vanilla. Combine flour, baking soda and salt; add to batter alternately with the buttermilk. In another mixing bowl, beat egg whites until soft peaks form. Fold into batter. Grease and flour one 8-in. round baking pan and one 13-in. x 9-in. x 2-in. baking pan. If desired, line bottoms with waxed paper; grease and flour paper. Pour 2-1/2 cups batter into round baking pan. Pour the remaining batter into the rectangular pan. Bake at 350° for 25-30 minutes (round) and 35-40 minutes (rectangular) or until a toothpick comes out clean. Cool in pans 10 minutes before removing to wire racks. Remove waxed paper and cool completely.

For frosting, combine sugar and cornstarch in a saucepan. Stir in milk and egg yolks until smooth. Add butter; bring to a boil over medium heat, stirring constantly until thickened and bubbly. Boil 2 minutes. Remove from the heat; stir in vanilla and coconut. Cool completely; set aside 3/4 cup. To remaining frosting, add green food coloring to obtain a grass color. Place rectangular cake on a serving platter; frost top and sides with green frosting. Place 1/2 cup vanilla frosting in a decorator tube; pipe 9-in. lines across cake for yard lines. Set tube aside.

For football, slice a 2-in.-wide strip from the center of round cake (save to eat later). Spread reserved coconut frosting on the bottom of one curved piece of cake; press the other piece against frosting. Place cut edge down on a flat surface.

Combine remaining vanilla frosting with cocoa; frost top and sides of football. Use decorator tube to pipe laces on football. With a large spatula, carefully lift football and place in center of green frosted cake.

Use three pipe cleaners at each end of cake to form goalposts as shown in the photo below. **Yield:** 20-24 servings.

Happy Clown Cake

(Pictured below and on page 98)

While this animated treat developed by our Test Kitchen staff is sure to bring about youthful grins, it'll also give Mom something to smile about. How's that? Cake mix, coconut, food coloring, purchased frosting and assorted candy are all you need to make it. Even serving the cake to birthday guests is a cinch. First, you pass out the cupcakes…then you cut up what's left!

> 1 package (18-1/4 ounces) yellow cake mix
> 1 cup flaked coconut, *divided*
> Yellow, blue, green and red food coloring
> 1 package (5 ounces) red shoestring licorice
> 1 can (16 ounces) vanilla frosting
> 2 mini peanut butter cups
> 1 package (2.17 ounces) Skittles bite-size candies

Mix cake batter according to package directions. Fill 12 paper-lined muffin cups two-thirds full. Pour remaining batter into a greased 9-in. round baking pan. Bake cake and cupcakes according to package directions. Cool 10 minutes; remove from pan. Cool completely.

Place 1/2 cup coconut in a plastic bag; sprinkle five to six drops of yellow food coloring into bag and shake until color is distributed evenly. Repeat with 1/4 cup coconut and blue coloring, then with remaining coconut and green coloring. Reserve one licorice piece for mouth; cut remaining pieces into 2-in. to 3-in. pieces for hair.

Frost round cake with vanilla frosting; place on a 22-in. x 15-in. serving board. Press peanut butter cups upside down in place for eyes. Form long licorice piece into mouth and press into frosting (insert a small piece for smile if desired).

Remove liner from one cupcake and cut the top off. Cut the top in half again and press into sides of frosted cake for ears. Tint 2 tablespoons of frosting with red food coloring; frost bottom half of cupcake and press in place for nose.

Frost all remaining cupcakes. Remove liners from two cupcakes and cut in half; sprinkle with green coconut. Press flat sides against top of cake to form brim of hat. Sprinkle five cupcakes with yellow coconut and one with blue coconut; stack in a pyramid on top of brim to make the hat.

Push ends of small licorice pieces into frosting for hair. Place remaining cupcakes at bottom of cake to make a bow tie; decorate those cupcakes with Skittles. **Yield:** 16-20 servings.

Dump Truck Cake

(Pictured at right and on page 98)

Gearing up to host a construction-themed birthday? This mouth-watering hauler will get your party on a roll! Our home economists made the treat speedy by using a packaged cake mix and spreading on easy-to-fix frosting. What's more, they formed the truck's shape with basic loaf pans instead of a special mold. You can

pave the way for your own big rig, too...just follow the simple instructions featured here!

1 package (18-1/4 ounces) chocolate cake mix
5 tablespoons plus 1 teaspoon shortening
5 tablespoons plus 1 teaspoon butter *or* margarine, softened
2-2/3 cups confectioners' sugar
2 tablespoons milk
3/4 teaspoon vanilla extract
Yellow and blue liquid food coloring
3 Ho-Ho snack cakes
6 chocolate-covered miniature doughnuts
Black shoestring licorice
2 large white gumdrops
2 red M&M's
1 milk chocolate candy bar (1.55 ounces)

Prepare cake mix according to package directions. Pour into two greased 8-in. x 4-in. x 2-in. loaf pans. Bake at 350° for 25-30 minutes or until a toothpick inserted near the center comes out clean. Cool for 10 minutes before removing from pans to wire racks to cool completely. Using a serrated knife, level the top of each cake. Crumble removed tops; set cakes and crumbs aside.

In a small mixing bowl, cream shortening and butter. Beat in confectioners' sugar, milk and vanilla. Place 1 cup frosting in a small bowl; tint yellow. Place 3/4 cup frosting in a bowl; tint blue. Place 1/4 cup frosting in a bowl; leave plain. Frost the top of one cake yellow; top with the remaining cake to form truck body.

For truck cab, measure 2 in. from one end. Cut 1-3/4 in. straight down; cut at an angle 1-1/2 in. deep and 1 in. toward the front of the truck. Remove cake wedge and save for another use.

For dump truck bed, leave 1-1/2 in. of cake for cab roof, then cut 1/2 in. deep at an angle. Make a horizontal cut to the back of the truck. Remove cake wedge and save for another use.

For wheel axles, place two snack cakes side by side and 1/2 in. apart near one corner of an 11-in. x 10-in. covered board. Place the remaining snack cake parallel to and 2 in. from the inside snack cake. Carefully arrange truck body over snack cakes. Frost the hood, doors and bottom third of the truck with yellow frosting. For wheels, attach doughnuts with plain frosting on each side of truck.

Spread some of the white frosting on the slanted windshield. Place the remaining white frosting in a pastry or plastic bag; cut a small hole in a corner. Pipe the windows on the doors. Frost the rest of the dump truck blue.

Cut thirteen 3/4-in. strips of licorice. Arrange eight strips on the front of the truck for the grille; set the remaining strips aside. For headlights, cut gumdrops in half. Place rounded half of each on outside of grille; discard the remaining cut gumdrops.

Cut two 3-1/2-in. strips, two 1-in. strips, six 1-3/4-in. strips, two 1-1/4-in. strips and four 2-in. strips of licorice. Using the 3-1/2-in. and 1-in. strips, form the windshield. Place two 3/4-in. strips on windshield for wipers. For doors, position two 1-1/4-in. strips for the door tops; place the 2-in. strips for the door sides. Decorate sides and back of truck with remaining licorice.

Place M&M's on back of bed for rear lights. For back bumper, break candy bar into individual sections at perforations. Cut one piece in half widthwise. Place some of the chocolate, flat side out, on the truck back (save remaining chocolate for another use).

Spoon reserved crumbled cake into truck bed for dirt.
Yield: 8-10 servings.

Buggy Gal Birthday Cake

LaVonne Hegland, St. Michael, Minnesota

(Pictured at right and on page 98)

Getting this confection off to a flying start is easy. Begin by baking LaVonne's delectably chocolate buttermilk cake in a bowl to form the buggy body. To create the colorful markings our Test Kitchen staff came up with, you can use purchased black frosting and a quick-to-make red version. Then dapple the ladybug with vanilla chips, licorice and peppermint patties for details. After following the step-by-step instructions that begin below, you'll be ready to set your own mouth-watering miss out on the table...and let folks start nibbling!

1 cup shortening
2 cups sugar
1 cup buttermilk
2 eggs
2-1/2 cups all-purpose flour
1/2 cup baking cocoa
2 teaspoons baking soda
1 teaspoon salt
1 cup water
FROSTING/DECORATING:
1/4 cup butter *or* margarine, softened
1/4 cup shortening
1/2 teaspoon vanilla extract
2 cups confectioners' sugar
4 to 5 teaspoons milk
Red paste food coloring
1 tube (4.25 ounces) black frosting (about 1/4 cup)
2 vanilla chips
12 chocolate-covered peppermint patties
2 pieces black shoestring licorice (2-1/2 inches)
Leaf-shaped spearmint gumdrops, optional

In a mixing bowl, cream shortening and sugar. Beat in milk and eggs. Combine flour, cocoa, baking soda and salt; add to the creamed mixture alternately with water. Pour into a greased and floured 4-qt. ovenproof bowl. Bake at 350° for 80-90 minutes (covering with foil halfway through baking time) or until a toothpick inserted near the center comes out clean. Cool for 10 minutes before removing from bowl to a wire rack to cool completely.

For frosting, cream butter, shortening and vanilla in a mixing bowl. Gradually beat in the sugar and enough milk to achieve a spreading consistency. Add food coloring. Set 3 tablespoons of frosting aside.

Place the cake on a serving platter. Frost with remaining frosting, leaving an 8-1/2-in. x 6-in. x 6-in. triangle of cake unfrosted. Frost the triangle with some of the black frosting. Fill a small bag with remaining black frosting; cut a small hole in corner of bag. Pipe a line from the tip of the triangle over the top of the cake to the other side, creating wings. With the same frosting, outline the edge of the triangle. For the eyes, pipe a 1/4-in. black dot on the flat side of each vanilla chip; position chips on black triangle and press gently into frosting.

Randomly place peppermint patties over red frosting for ladybug's spots; press down gently. Fill a small bag

with reserved red frosting; cut a small hole in corner of bag. Pipe a smile under eyes. Insert licorice pieces above eyes for antennae. Place gumdrops around the edge of the platter if desired. **Yield:** 12-16 servings.

Chicken Cake

(Pictured at right)

From its fruit roll-up comb to its licorice legs, this sweet treat is more than just chicken feed! It's a delectable dessert fit for an "egg-stra" fun birthday. You can make the feathered confection by shaping round cakes using a packaged mix like our Test Kitchen home economists did. Then spread on homemade frosting and add goodies for decorations.

1 package (18-1/4 ounces) yellow cake mix
3 tablespoons all-purpose flour
1 cup milk
1/2 cup butter *or* margarine, softened
1/2 cup shortening
1 cup sugar
1 teaspoon vanilla extract
4 cream-filled sponge cakes
4 lemon-flavored *or* black licorice twists
Black shoestring licorice (15 inches)
2 chocolate-covered peanut butter candies
1 red fruit roll-up

Prepare cake batter according to package directions. Divide between six greased muffin cups, a greased 10-oz. custard cup and a greased 8-in. round baking pan. Bake at 350° for 15-25 minutes or until a toothpick inserted near the center comes out clean. Cool cupcakes for 5 minutes and cakes for 10 minutes before removing from pans to wire racks to cool completely.

In a saucepan, whisk flour and milk until smooth. Bring to a boil; cook and stir for 2 minutes or until thickened. Cool. In a mixing bowl, cream butter, shortening, sugar and vanilla. Beat in milk mixture until sugar is dissolved, about 4 minutes.

On a 17-in.-square covered board, place 8-in. cake for chicken's body with small cake above it for head. For wings, split sponge cakes in half widthwise; place four on each side of large cake. Frost tops and sides of cakes and tops of cupcakes. Arrange cupcakes randomly around board or serve separately.

For legs, cut two licorice twists into 12-in. pieces and place below large cake. For beak, cut a 1/4-in. triangle of licorice; center on bottom third of head.

Cut remaining licorice twists into 1-1/2-in. slices; cut one end of 16 of the slices at an angle. For chicken feet, arrange one diagonally sliced licorice piece on each side of legs, straight edge down. Place one straight-cut licorice piece in the center of each cupcake; arrange remaining diagonally sliced pieces on each side.

Shape black shoestring licorice into glasses; press gently into frosting to hold the shape. Add chocolate-covered candies for eyes.

For chicken's comb, cut fruit roll-up into a 3-in. strip. Cutting along a long edge of the roll-up, make three connecting semicircles. Gently press strip, flat side toward cake, onto top of head. **Yield:** 12-15 servings.

INDEX

This handy index lists each recipe by major ingredients. For specific types of cakes, refer to the recipe list at the beginning of each chapter.